ENERGY POLICIES, POLITICS AND PRICES

U.S. CRUDE OIL EXPORTS

RESTRICTIONS AND CONSIDERATIONS

ENERGY POLICIES, POLITICS AND PRICES

Additional books in this series can be found on Nova's website under the Series tab.

Additional e-books in this series can be found on Nova's website under the e-book tab.

ENERGY POLICIES, POLITICS AND PRICES

U.S. CRUDE OIL EXPORTS

RESTRICTIONS AND CONSIDERATIONS

MICHAEL POPE
EDITOR

New York

Library of Congress Cataloging-in-Publication Data

ISBN: 978-1-63463-070-2

Published by Nova Science Publishers, Inc. † New York

CONTENTS

Preface		**vii**
Chapter 1	U.S. Crude Oil Export Policy: Background and Considerations *Phillip Brown, Robert Pirog, Adam Vann, Ian F. Fergusson, Michael Ratner and Jonathan L. Ramseur*	**1**
Chapter 2	Testimony of Amy Myers Jaffe, Executive Director of Energy and Sustainability, Institute of Transportation Studies, University of California, Davis. Hearing on "U.S. Crude Oil Exports: Opportunities and Challenges"	**43**
Chapter 3	Statement of Harold Hamm, Chairman and CEO, Continental Resources, Inc. Hearing on "U.S. Crude Oil Exports: Opportunities and Challenges"	**55**
Chapter 4	Testimony of Graeme Burnett, Senior Vice President, Delta Air Lines. Hearing on "U.S. Crude Oil Exports: Opportunities and Challenges"	**61**
Chapter 5	Testimony of Daniel J. Weiss, Senior Fellow and Director of Climate Strategy, Center for American Progress. Hearing on "U.S. Crude Oil Exports: Opportunities and Challenges"	**65**
Index		**71**

PREFACE

As a result of advanced oil drilling and extraction technologies (primarily horizontal drilling and hydraulic fracturing), crude oil production in the United States is growing and, according to Energy Information Administration (EIA) reference case projections, may reach 9.6 million barrels per day by 2019. Production of light tight oil (LTO) is, and is expected to be, the primary contributor to U.S. crude oil production growth in the near to medium term. This book provides background and context about the crude oil legal and regulatory framework, discusses motivations that underlie the desire to export U.S. crude oil, and presents analysis of issues that Congress may choose to consider during debate about U.S. crude oil export policy.

Chapter 1 – During an era of oil price controls and following the 1973 Organization of Arab Petroleum Exporting Countries oil embargo, Congress passed the Energy Policy and Conservation Act of 1975 (EPCA), which directs the President "to promulgate a rule prohibiting the export of crude oil" produced in the United States. Crude oil export restrictions are codified in the Export Administration Regulations administered by the Bureau of Industry and Security (BIS)—a Commerce Department agency. The President has some powers to allow certain crude oil exports if an exemption is determined to be in the national interest.

In 2009, a decades-long U.S. oil production decline was reversed due to the application of advanced drilling and extraction technologies to produce tight oil. The Energy Information Administration (EIA) 2014 reference case projects that total U.S. crude production will be 9.6 million barrels per day by 2019—up from 7.7 million in 2013. Nearly all of this growth is expected to come from tight oil production. This anticipated growth is resulting in calls to lift or otherwise ease U.S. crude oil export restrictions. However, crude oil imports are projected to range from 6 million to nearly 8 million barrels per day for the period out to 2040. This apparent disconnect between import needs and the desire to export can be explained when considering the following: (1) geographic location of tight oil, (2) tight oil quality characteristics, (3) refinery configurations, (4) oil transportation network, and (5) price discounts in different regions.

EIA's reference case also projects that tight oil production will decline after 2019, raising questions about the potentially temporary nature of the export opportunity. However, EIA's high-growth case projects tight oil production growth out to 2040. There is a degree of uncertainty associated with long-term tight oil projections.

Tight oil produced in the United States is generally of the light/sweet (low sulfur) variety, referred to as light tight oil (LTO). Expected LTO volumes could potentially result in an oversupply of light crudes in certain regions, such as the Gulf Coast where refineries are currently configured to process heavy/sour crudes and yield certain volumes of specific oil products (e.g., diesel and gasoline). Timing for a potential LTO oversupply situation is uncertain. Some analysts estimate that it could occur as early as 2015. However, the oil industry is dynamic. It will adjust based on market and economic considerations (e.g., price discounts, product values, and investment requirements). For example, refineries can add equipment to process additional light crude volumes. Transportation modes (i.e., pipeline, rail, and marine vessels) can adapt to deliver LTO to refineries throughout the country. While investments in equipment could allow refiners to process more LTO, economic considerations will likely dictate how much additional LTO will be absorbed domestically. Condensate, an extra-light hydrocarbon, is of particular concern to some oil producers because of its limited domestic marketability, increasing production volumes, and inclusion in the BIS crude oil definition.

There are several issues that Congress may consider associated with exporting U.S. crude oil. Of particular interest may be how allowing exports might affect crude oil prices. These effects are likely to be threefold: (1) domestic prices for exported oil will likely converge towards the world price, (2) U.S. benchmark prices will likely adjust to world prices, and (3) world prices will likely adjust to reflect added supplies. The magnitude of these price effects will depend on export volumes. Product price (i.e., gasoline) effects may be mixed and could differ by region. Additional considerations that may be of interest to Congress might include potential impacts on energy security, geopolitics, international trade, and the environment.

Multiple crude oil export policy options might be considered that range from lifting current export restrictions to maintaining export restrictions.

Additionally, there are several other policy options that might include exempting LTO from export restrictions, modifying the BIS crude oil definition, or allowing crude oil exports for a limited period of time.

Chapter 2 – This is Testimony of Amy Myers Jaffe, Executive Director of Energy and Sustainability, Institute of Transportation Studies, University of California, Davis. Hearing on "U.S. Crude Oil Exports: Opportunities and Challenges" before the Senate Committee on Energy and Natural Resources, dated January 30, 2014.

Chapter 3 – This is Statement of Harold Hamm, Chairman and CEO, Continental Resources, Inc. Hearing on "U.S. Crude Oil Exports: Opportunities and Challenges" before the Senate Committee on Energy and Natural Resources, dated January 30, 2014.

Chapter 4 – This is Testimony of Graeme Burnett, Senior Vice President, Delta Air Lines. Hearing on "U.S. Crude Oil Exports: Opportunities and Challenges" before the Senate Committee on Energy and Natural Resources, January 30, 2014.

Chapter 5 – This is Testimony of Daniel J. Weiss, Senior Fellow and Director of Climate Strategy, Center for American Progress. Hearing on "U.S. Crude Oil Exports: Opportunities and Challenges" before the Senate Committee on Energy and Natural Resources, January 30, 2014.

In: U.S. Crude Oil Exports
Editor: Michael Pope

ISBN: 978-1-63463-070-2

Chapter 1

U.S. CRUDE OIL EXPORT POLICY: BACKGROUND AND CONSIDERATIONS*

Phillip Brown, Robert Pirog, Adam Vann, Ian F. Fergusson, Michael Ratner and Jonathan L. Ramseur

SUMMARY

During an era of oil price controls and following the 1973 Organization ofArab Petroleum Exporting Countries oil embargo, Congress passed the Energy Policy and Conservation Act of 1975 (EPCA), which directs the President "to promulgate a rule prohibiting the export of crude oil" produced in the United States. Crude oil export restrictions are codified in the Export Administration Regulations administered by the Bureau of Industry and Security (BIS)—a Commerce Department agency. The President has some powers to allow certain crude oil exports if an exemption is determined to be in the national interest.

In 2009, a decades-long U.S. oil production decline was reversed due to the application of advanced drilling and extraction technologies to produce tight oil. The Energy Information Administration (EIA) 2014 reference case

* This is an edited, reformatted and augmented version of a Congressional Research Service publication R43442, prepared for Members and Committees of Congress dated March 26, 2014.

projects that total U.S. crude production will be 9.6 million barrels per day by 2019—up from 7.7 million in 2013. Nearly all of this growth is expected to come from tight oil production. This anticipated growth is resulting in calls to lift or otherwise ease U.S. crude oil export restrictions. However, crude oil imports are projected to range from 6 million to nearly 8 million barrels per day for the period out to 2040. This apparent disconnect between import needs and the desire to export can be explained when considering the following: (1) geographic location of tight oil, (2) tight oil quality characteristics, (3) refinery configurations, (4) oil transportation network, and (5) price discounts in different regions.

EIA's reference case also projects that tight oil production will decline after 2019, raising questions about the potentially temporary nature of the export opportunity. However, EIA's high-growth case projects tight oil production growth out to 2040. There is a degree of uncertainty associated with long-term tight oil projections.

Tight oil produced in the United States is generally of the light/sweet (low sulfur) variety, referred to as light tight oil (LTO). Expected LTO volumes could potentially result in an oversupply of light crudes in certain regions, such as the Gulf Coast where refineries are currently configured to process heavy/sour crudes and yield certain volumes of specific oil products (e.g., diesel and gasoline). Timing for a potential LTO oversupply situation is uncertain. Some analysts estimate that it could occur as early as 2015. However, the oil industry is dynamic. It will adjust based on market and economic considerations (e.g., price discounts, product values, and investment requirements). For example, refineries can add equipment to process additional light crude volumes. Transportation modes (i.e., pipeline, rail, and marine vessels) can adapt to deliver LTO to refineries throughout the country. While investments in equipment could allow refiners to process more LTO, economic considerations will likely dictate how much additional LTO will be absorbed domestically. Condensate, an extra-light hydrocarbon, is of particular concern to some oil producers because of its limited domestic marketability, increasing production volumes, and inclusion in the BIS crude oil definition.

There are several issues that Congress may consider associated with exporting U.S. crude oil. Of particular interest may be how allowing exports might affect crude oil prices. These effects are likely to be threefold: (1) domestic prices for exported oil will likely converge towards the world price, (2) U.S. benchmark prices will likely adjust to world prices, and (3) world prices will likely adjust to reflect added supplies. The magnitude of these price effects will depend on export volumes. Product price (i.e., gasoline) effects may be mixed and could differ by region. Additional considerations that may be of interest to Congress might include potential impacts on energy security, geopolitics, international trade, and the environment.

Multiple crude oil export policy options might be considered that range from lifting current export restrictions to maintaining export restrictions. Additionally, there are several other policy options that might include exempting LTO from export restrictions, modifying the BIS crude oil definition, or allowing crude oil exports for a limited period of time.

INTRODUCTION

As a result of advanced oil drilling and extraction technologies (primarily horizontal drilling and hydraulic fracturing), crude oil production in the United States is growing and, according to Energy Information Administration (EIA) reference case projections, may reach 9.6 million barrels per day (bbl/d) by 2019—up from 5 million bbl/d in 2008 (see **Figure 1**).[1] Production of light tight oil (LTO) is, and is expected to be, the primary contributor to U.S. crude oil production growth in the near to medium term. As U.S. LTO production has increased, some have called for crude oil export restrictions to be either eased or lifted altogether.[2] However, according to the Energy Information Administration (EIA), U.S. crude oil demand is forecasted to be approximately 15 million bbl/d through 2040.[3] According to EIA's reference case, crude oil imports are projected to range between 6 million and 8 million bbl/d over the same period.[4] Although, EIA's high resource case projections, if realized, could result in lower import requirements. This apparent disconnect between expected import needs and the desire to export crude oil can be explained when considering the following: (1) the geographical location of LTO production, (2) the type/quality (i.e., light, sweet) of crude oil being produced, (3) the types of crude oil that some U.S. refineries are currently configured to optimally refine, (4) the petroleum products that are derived from different types of crude oil, and (5) transportation and infrastructure challenges associated with moving certain types of crude oil to demand centers. Each of these aspects is discussed in more detail throughout this report.

While U.S. crude oil exports are restricted under current law, petroleum products such as naphtha[5], gasoline, diesel fuel, and natural gas liquids are not subject to export restrictions. As a result, production and export of these products have increased in recent years. In October 2013, approximately 3.8

million barrels per day (bbl/d) of petroleum products were exported from the United States—up from an average of nearly 1.4 million bbl/d in 2007.[6]

Members of Congress have taken various positions regarding crude oil exports, including (1) calling for the Administration to lift export restrictions,[7] (2) maintaining existing restrictions,[8] and (3) opposing attempts to lift restrictions through the World Trade Organization.[9]

The crude oil export policy debate has multiple dimensions and complexities. As U.S. LTO production has increased—along with additional oil supply from Canada—certain challenges have emerged that affect some oil producers and refiners. While the economic arguments both for and against U.S. crude oil exports are quite complex and dynamic, there are some fundamental concepts and issues that may be worth considering during debate about exporting U.S. crude oil.

This report provides background and context about the crude oil legal and regulatory framework, discusses motivations that underlie the desire to export U.S. crude oil, and presents analysis of issues that Congress may choose to consider during debate about U.S. crude oil export policy.

BACKGROUND

Current crude oil export restrictions date back to the 1970s, during an era of U.S. oil price controls that motivated producers to export and sell crude oil at unregulated world prices.[10] In response, crude oil, petroleum products, and natural gas liquids were placed on the Commodity Control List established by the Export Administration Act of 1969.[11] In 1973, the Organization of Arab Petroleum Exporting Countries (OAPEC) imposed a total embargo of crude oil delivered to the United States.[12] The oil embargo motivated Congress to enact laws that would limit U.S. crude oil export opportunities.[13] The embargo resulted in rapid and steep crude oil price increases, thereby creating a perception of oil resource scarcity and prompting concerns about U.S. crude oil import reliance.[14] In response to these concerns Congress passed legislation—including the Energy Policy and Conservation Act (EPCA)—to restrict U.S. crude oil exports, with some exceptions as determined by the President. Using these exceptions, the United States has exported crude oil for decades, although in relatively low volumes. Crude oil exports reached a level of 287,000 bbl/d in 1980.[15] In 2013, crude oil exports from the United States averaged 120,000 bbl/d, almost all of which was sent to Canada.[16]

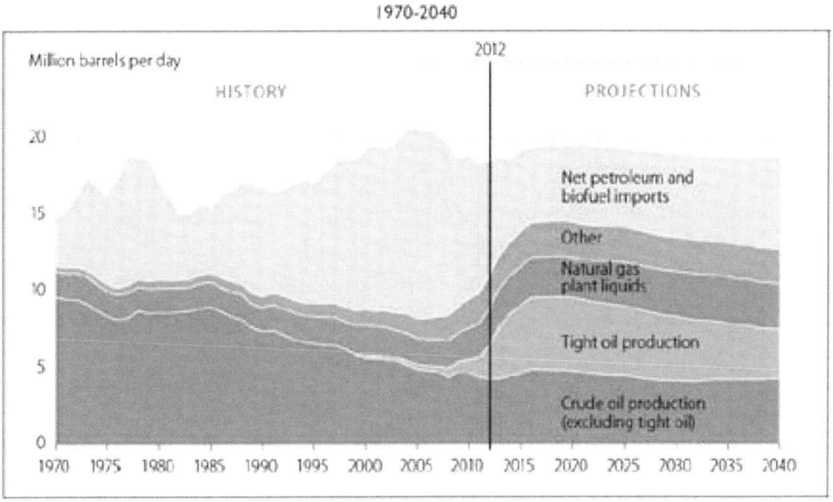

Source: Energy Information Administration, Annual Energy Outlook 2014 Reference Case Early Release Overview.

Figure 1. U.S. Petroleum and Other Liquid Fuels Supply by Source 1970-2040.

In the context of exports, the Bureau of Industry and Security (BIS)—the Department of Commerce agency responsible for crude oil export licenses—defines "crude oil" as follows:

> "Crude oil" is defined as a mixture of hydrocarbons that existed in liquid phase in underground reservoirs and remains liquid at atmospheric pressure after passing through surface separating facilities and which has not been processed through a crude oil distillation tower. Included are reconstituted crude petroleum, and lease condensate and liquid hydrocarbons produced from tar sands, gilsonite, and oil shale. Drip gases are also included, but topped crude oil, residual oil, and other finished and unfinished oils are excluded.[17]

From 1970 to 2008, U.S. crude oil production was on a steady decline (see **Figure 1**). During this time, there were periods when easing crude oil export restrictions was a national-level policy topic and presidential determinations were made to exempt crude oil exports that met certain criteria. In 2009, production of light/sweet crude in tight oil formations throughout the country started to increase rapidly, and production levels are expected to continue rising out to 2019, or perhaps later.

The physical and chemical properties of LTO, when placed into context of the crude oil slate[18] desired by U.S. refineries, is one important factor that underlies the crude oil export debate. For more information about crude oil characteristics, see the text box below.

Prior to the advent of advanced drilling and extraction technologies, many U.S. refiners in the Midwest and Gulf Coast invested in equipment to process heavy crudes from Canada and Latin America. Generally, these investments were encouraged by price discounts for heavy crudes.

Tight oil production has changed the situation and the entire industry is adjusting. Investments are being made to process more light crude. Transportation bottlenecks are being relieved. However, as LTO volumes increase, oil producers are bracing for continuing price discounts that may result from a structural oversupply of light crudes in certain regions. Whether the industry will be economically motivated to continue adjusting to accommodate expected light crude production and supply is uncertain.

LEGAL AND REGULATORY CONTEXT

The export of domestically produced crude oil has been significantly restricted since the 1970s by an array of federal laws and regulations, in particular the Energy Policy and Conservation Act of 1975 (EPCA)[20] and the resultant Short Supply Control Regulations adopted and administered by the Bureau of Industry and Security (BIS). These laws and regulations are discussed below.

The Energy Policy and Conservation Act

EPCA directs the President to "promulgate a rule prohibiting the export of crude oil and natural gas produced in the United States, except that the President may ... exempt from such prohibition such crude oil or natural gas exports which he determines to be consistent with the national interest and the purposes of this chapter."[21] The act further provides that the exemptions to the prohibition should be "based on the purpose for export, class of seller or purchaser, country of destination, or any other reasonable classification or basis as the President determines to be appropriate and consistent with the national interest and the purposes of this chapter."[22]

ALL CRUDE OIL IS NOT CREATED EQUAL

Hundreds of different types of crude oil are produced globally, each of which has unique qualities and characteristics. Two of the most common parameters used to compare different types of crude oil are (1) API gravity, and (2) sulfur content. API gravity, expressed in degrees, indicates the density of crude oil.

The higher the API gravity, the lighter the crude oil. Sulfur content, expressed as a percentage, indicates the amount of sulfur contained in a particular crude stream. High sulfur content crudes are referred to as "sour" and low sulfur content crudes are referred to as "sweet."[19] Additionally, when processed by a refinery, different crude oils can yield varying amounts of petroleum products such as gasoline, diesel fuel, jet fuel, and fuel oil. The following table compares five different types of crude oil based on API, sulfur content, and initial product yield.

			Initial Product Yield (%)				
Crude Oil (Yr)	**API°**	**Sulfur (%)**	**Resid**	**Gas oil**	**Distillate**	**Naphtha**	**Other**
Maya ('07)	20.5 (H)	3.65 (Sr)	36	14	21	18	1
Arabian Heavy ('01)	27.5 (H)	2.78 (Sr)	30	25	24	18	3
Eagle Ford Cond. ('11)	55.6 (XL)	0.01 (Swt)	1	15	31	48	5
Eagle Ford 40 ('12)	40.1 (L)	0.09 (Swt)	11	28	33	26	2
West Texas Sour ('01)	32.4 (M)	1.72 (Sr)	14	29	29	27	1

Source: API and Sulfur numbers from EIA; Product Yields from Chevron Assays.

Notes: Product yields represent typical initial yields off atmospheric and vacuum towers, which is generally the first step in the refining process. Additional processing steps (i.e., cracking, coking, combining, etc.) are used to produce finished products such as gasoline, diesel fuel, and others. Individual refineries are typically configured to handle a certain blend of crude oils that will produce an optimized volume of initial and finished products. H = Heavy; M = Medium; L = Light; XL = Extra Light; Sr = Sour; Swt = Sweet; Cond. = condensate.

Definitions: (1) *Resid* represents residual fuel oil, which is a general classification for heavier oils that can be used as feedstock for a coking refinery;

(2) *Gas* oil refers to fuel oils that are lighter than resid but heavier than distillate and can include certain heating oils and fuels; (3) *Distillate* can be used as either a diesel fuel or a fuel oil; (4) *Naphtha* can be blended with other materials to produce motor gasoline or jet fuel. Naphtha can also be used as a solvent or as a petrochemical feedstock; (5) *Other* generally refers to light refinery gases such as butane and propane.

Oil refiners, which process a blend of different crude oils, generally look to optimize the type/quality of crude streams to produce the desired product (i.e., gasoline and diesel fuel) output based on price (crude oil prices and product values) and other market conditions. The technical configuration, product markets, and economic conditions for each individual refinery will affect the desired crude oil selection.

This general prohibition on crude oil exports and the exemptions to that prohibition mandated by EPCA are found in the BIS regulations on Short Supply Controls at 15 C.F.R. §754.2. The regulations provide that a license must be obtained for all exports of crude oil, including those to Canada.[23] There are enumerated exceptions to the license requirement for foreign origin crude oil stored in the Strategic Petroleum Reserves,[24] small samples exported for analytic and testing purposes,[25] and exports of oil transported by pipeline over rights-of-way granted pursuant to Section 203 of the Trans-Alaska Pipeline AuthorizationAct.[26]

The regulations provide that BIS will issue licenses for certain crude oil exports that fall under one of the listed exemptions, including (1) exports from Alaska's Cook Inlet; (2) exports to Canada for consumption or use therein; (3) exports in connection with refining or exchange of Strategic Petroleum Reserve oil; (4) exports of heavy California crude oil up to an average volume not to exceed 25,000 barrels per day; (5) exports that are consistent with certain international agreements; (6) exports that are consistent with findings made by the President under certain statutes (see section below titled "Other Relevant Federal Statutes"); and (7) exports of foreign origin crude oil where, based on satisfactory written documentation, the exporter can demonstrate that the oil is not of U.S. origin and has not been commingled with oil of U.S. origin.[27]

The regulations also direct BIS to review applications to export crude oil that do not fall under one of these exemptions on a "case by case basis" and to approve such applications on a finding that the proposed export is "consistent with the national interest and the purposes of the Energy Policy and

Conservation Act."[28] However, the regulations suggest that only certain specific exports will be authorized pursuant to this case-by-case review. The regulations provide that while BIS "will consider all applications for approval," generally BIS will only approve those applications that are either for temporary exports (e.g., a pipeline that crosses an international border before returning to the United States), or are for transactions (1) that result directly in importation of an equal or greater quantity and quality of crude oil; (2) that take place under contracts that can be terminated if petroleum supplies of the United States are threatened; and (3) for which the applicant can demonstrate that for compelling economic or technological reasons, the crude oil cannot reasonably be marketed in the United States[29]

The Export Administration Act and the International Emergency Economic Powers Act

Although EPCA directs the President to promulgate regulations that restrict crude oil exports, it does not provide the regulatory framework for enforcement of that restriction and the issuance of licenses for eligible exports. As mentioned above, the BIS is tasked with that duty, which is handled under its "short supply control" regulations. The source of this authority is somewhat complicated. The Export Administration Act of 1979 (EAA)[30] confers upon the President the power to control exports for national security, foreign policy, or short-supply purposes, authorizes the President to establish export licensing mechanisms for certain items, and provides guidance and places certain limits on that authority.[31] These restrictions are enforced by BIS. Crude oil restrictions and licensing are found in the BIS short supply controls authorized by the EAA.

However, the EAA expired in August 2001. The provisions of the act, and the regulations issued pursuant to it, remain in effect via yearly executive orders issued by the President under authority granted to him by the International Emergency Economic Powers Act.[32] That act authorizes the President to "deal with any unusual and extraordinary threat, which has its source in whole or substantial part outside the United States, to the national security, foreign policy, or economy of the United States, if the President declares a national emergency with respect to such threat."[33] When the EAA first expired in 2001, the President cited this emergency authority in the issuance of Executive Order 13222, which provided for the continued execution of the EAA and the regulations issued pursuant to it.[34] This exercise of emergency authority has been repeated annually by the President since that time, most recently in August 2013.[35]

Other Relevant Federal Statutes

In addition to the statutes described above, several other federal statutes either bar certain types of crude oil exports or mandate that certain crude oil exports be exempt from the general prohibition in EPCA.

Section 201 of P.L. 104-58: Exports of Alaskan North Slope Oil

Section 201 of P.L. 104-58 amended the Mineral Leasing Act (MLA),[36] to authorize the export of oil transported by pipeline over the right-of-way granted pursuant to the Trans-Alaska Pipeline Authorization Act unless the President finds that export of this oil is not in the national interest.[37] The President's national interest determination must, at a minimum, consider (1) whether the export will diminish the quantity or quality of petroleum available in the United States; (2) the results of an environmental review; and (3) whether the export might cause sustained material oil supply shortages or significantly increase oil prices above world market levels.[38] The legislation required submission of this national interest determination within five months of November 28, 1995.[39]

In April 1996, President Clinton issued a determination that such exports were in the national interest.[40] BIS administers authorizations of Trans-Alaska Pipeline System oil exports pursuant to 15 C.F.R. §754.2(j), which carves out an exception to the general crude oil export licensing requirements provided that certain conditions regarding the physical transportation of the crude oil are satisfied.

MLA Limitation on Export of Crude Oil Transported via Federal Right-of-Way

Section 28(u) of the MLA clarifies that all domestically produced crude oil (except oil exchanged for similar quantities for purposes of convenience or efficiency) transported through federal lands via rights-of-way granted pursuant to the MLA "shall be subject to all of the limitations and licensing requirements of the Export Administration Act."[41] Section 28(u) also provides that before such exports may occur, the President must "make and publish an express finding that such exports will not diminish the total quantity or quality of petroleum available in the United States, and are in the national interest and are in accord with the provisions of the Export Administration Act."[42] The

MLA further directs the President to submit reports to Congress containing these findings, and provides that Congress "shall have a period of sixty days, thirty days of which Congress must have been in session, to consider whether exports under the terms of this section are in the national interest. If Congress ... passes a concurrent resolution of disapproval stating disagreement with the President's finding concerning the national interest, further exports ... shall cease."[43] The MLArestriction on exports of crude oil that are transported through federal lands via a right-of-way is incorporated into the BIS regulations at 15 C.F.R. §754.2(c)(ii).

Limitation on Export of Oil from the Naval Petroleum Reserves

10 U.S.C. §7430(e) provides that petroleum produced at the naval petroleum reserves (except petroleum exchanged for similar quantities for purposes of convenience or efficiency) "shall be subject to all of the limitations and licensing requirements of the Export Administration Act." Section 7430(e) also provides that before such exports can take place, the President must "make and publish an express finding that such exports will not diminish the total quantity or quality of petroleum available in the United States, and are in the national interest and are in accord with the provisions of the ExportAdministration Act."[44] The Section 7430(e) restriction on exports of petroleum produced at the naval petroleum reserves is incorporated into the BIS regulations at 15 C.F.R. §754.2(c)(iv).

Limitation on Export of Crude Oil Produced from the Outer Continental Shelf

Section 28 of the Outer Continental Shelf Lands Act (OCSLA)[45] provides that any oil or gas produced from the Outer Continental Shelf (OCS)[46] "shall be subject to all of the limitations and licensing requirements of the Export Administration Act." As with the statutory export limitations discussed above, exports meeting this description are only authorized if the President makes "an express finding that such exports will not increase reliance on imported oil or gas, are in the national interest, and are in accord with the provisions of the Export AdministrationAct."[47] The OCSLA requires the President to submit reports containing such findings to Congress and provides that Congress "shall have a period of sixty calendar days, thirty days of which Congress must have been in session, to consider whether exports under the terms of this section are in the national interest. If the Congress ... passes a concurrent resolution of disapproval stating disagreement with the President's finding concerning the national interest, further exports ... shall cease."[48] The OCSLA restriction on exports of petroleum produced from the OCS is incorporated into the BIS regulations at 15 C.F.R. §754.2(c)(iii).

The Role of the Bureau of Industry and Security (BIS)

As noted above, exports of crude oil are licensed under the short supply controls of the Export Administration Act. The Export Administration Regulations (EAR) codify the requirements and provisions of the various statutes, which are administered by the Bureau of Industry and Security. Except in certain instances, a license is required for the export of crude oil from the United States.

License applications are examined by the Office of National Security and Technology Transfer Controls at BIS. Only a U.S. exporter or entity may apply for a license. License applications are made electronically, thus one must register on the BIS Simplified NetworkApplication Process Redesign (SNAP-R).[49] Once registered, the applicant must list the exporter, consignee, the volume of the export and its monetary value, a description of the product, its end-use, and a certification of origin for the product.

All BIS license applications are handled according to Executive Order 12981. Within nine days, BIS must contact the applicant if additional information is required; return without action if additional information is required or if a license is not needed; or refer the application to another agency. Once an application has been submitted, BIS has 30 days to make a decision. However, unlike dual-use technology licenses, crude oil licenses are not referred to other agencies. Thus, most crude oil licenses are handled within a 7-10 day period. A license is good for one year and is non-transferable, unless it is part of the assets of a company being bought or sold.

Certain crude oil exports can be shipped with a license exception. A license exception is an authorization to export or re-export, under certain conditions, items subject to the EAR that normally would require a license. Basically, under a license exception, the exporter certifies that a lawful transaction is taking place while maintaining proper documentation. The three license exceptions available for crude oil exports are (1) shipments of foreign-origin crude stored in the Strategic Petroleum Reserve; (2) shipments of samples for analytic or testing purposes; and (3) Trans-Alaska pipeline shipments. In order to use the TAPS license exception, certain tanker routing and environmental restrictions must be observed. Additionally, vessels used to export TAPS crude oil must be U.S.-owned and crewed. In addition, the licenses allow no re-exports, thus, prohibiting, for example, trans-shipments to foreign destinations through Canada.

The number of crude oil license applications has steadily increased over the last few years, from 31 applications in FY2008 to 103 in FY2013 (see **Table A-1** in **Appendix A** for additional detail). In the last several years, no licenses have been rejected, although some have been returned without action. This high approval rate is likely due to the specificity and exporters' knowledge of the regulations. The vast majority of licenses are for exports to Canada. For countries other than Canada, the exports can be attributed to re-exports of foreign crude oil that has not been commingled with domestic crude.

CRUDE OIL EXPORT MOTIVATIONS

As tight oil production has rapidly increased, technical and economic factors are motivating some stakeholders to pursue lifting crude oil export restrictions. Some oil producers would like to receive higher prices for oil produced. However, some refiners are concerned that regional crude oil acquisition price discounts may narrow if exports are expanded. Narrow price discounts may affect refinery operating margins and may result in some refineries ceasing operations. Additionally, some refiners may need to consider capital investments necessary to absorb increasing volumes of LTO—along with the value of products yielded from refining LTO. As mentioned above, the geographic location of tight oil production, refinery configurations, infrastructure limitations, and prices received by some oil producers have been cited as justification for lifting export restrictions. However, it is important to realize that these factors are not static in nature. Rather, they are dynamic and are constantly changing. Refineries can adjust their operations. Transportation infrastructure can adjust based on market conditions. Therefore, oil values received by oil producers would likely adjust as well. In 2013, the Energy Information Administration stated:

> Some recent commentary has suggested that it was likely or even inevitable that the growth in U.S. oil production from tight resources would be significantly curtailed unless there was a relaxation of current U.S. policies toward crude oil exports. However, this is likely an overstatement of the actual situation, because there are several other

midstream and downstream adjustments that could help to accommodate changing production patterns.[50]

The dynamic nature of the oil industry makes the debate about oil export policy inherently complex. Each of the three primary industry segments—production, transportation, and refining—will adjust based on changes to any one of the other segments. As a result, it can be difficult to assess the potential impacts of policy decisions on any one segment without considering how the other two might adjust to changing market conditions. With that caveat, additional detail about some of the motivations for crude oil exports is provided in the following sections.

Tight Oil Production Has Increased

In 2000, approximately 250,000 bbl/d of tight oil was produced in the United States.[51] In 2012, U.S. tight oil production was 2.25 million bbl/day, a nearly 10-fold increase.[52] The Energy Information Administration (EIA) 2014 reference case projects that U.S. tight oil production will continue to increase in the near to medium term and projects that LTO production may peak at 4.8 million bbl/day in 2019.[53] Most of this production is expected to come from three tight oil formations: (1) Eagle Ford in Texas, (2) Permian Basin in Texas, and (3) Bakken in North Dakota (see **Figure 2**). It is important to note that EIA projections for LTO production are subject to assumptions that are based on currently available information and current policies (e.g., export restrictions). These projections would likely change over time as new information becomes available and if policies are modified. Some degree of uncertainty exists in terms of how much LTO might be produced. Future projections may be either higher or lower than those included in EIA's 2014 Annual Energy Outlook.

Timing for a potential oversupply, and resulting price discounts, of U.S. LTO is also uncertain and depends on several factors. Some analysts estimate that price discounts related to the combination of LTO production volumes and export restrictions may occur as early as 2015/2016 or sometime after 2020.[54] Some of the factors that will likely impact the timing and magnitude of price discounts include (1) actual LTO production levels, (2) potential for U.S. exports to Canada, (3) LTO access to West Coast markets, (4) potential to displace light sour and medium grade crudes in refineries, and (5) the amount of additional LTO processing capacity at refineries.[55]

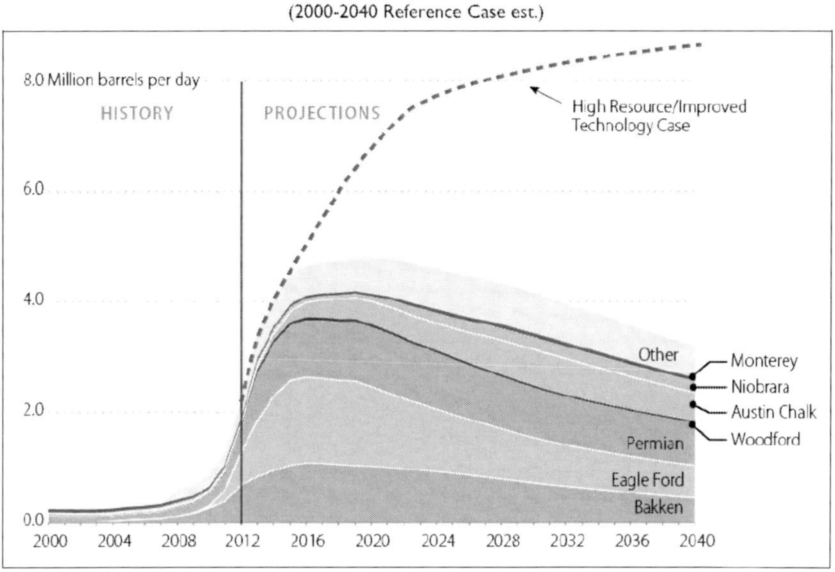

Source: Energy Information Administration, Annual Energy Outlook 2014 Early Release. High Resource/Improved Technology Case preliminary projections were provided by EIA and are used with permission.

Notes: The area chart shows EIA's reference case projections for tight oil production by formation. The red dashed line shows EIA's high resource/improved technology case for total tight oil production out to 2040. The disparity between these two projections illustrates some of the uncertainty associated with long-term tight oil production in the United States. Locations for tight oil formations are as follows: Bakken, North Dakota; Eagle Ford, Texas; Permian, Texas and New Mexico; Woodford, Oklahoma; Austin Chalk, Texas, Louisiana, and Mississippi; Niobrara, Colorado and Wyoming; Monterey, California.

Figure 2. U.S.Tight Oil Production, by Formation.

Based on EIA reference case projections in **Figure 2**, LTO production is projected to rapidly increase and peak around 2019. The implication of the reference case production profile is that the window of opportunity for crude oil exports—depending on export volumes—may be temporary. The potential temporary nature of the export opportunity may reflect the continuous and rapid drilling that may be needed to maintain and increase LTO volumes. Although, EIA's preliminary High Resource case indicates that LTO may continue growing out to 2040. As noted above, actual and projected production can, and does, change over time. The High Resource case reflects how industry knowledge could expand and technologies could improve, thereby resulting in increased U.S. LTO production in the future. LTO production at scale is a relatively new industry development and, thus, it is likely too early to accurately predict the magnitude of future production levels.

One element of LTO production is the increase in extremely light hydrocarbons that might be classified as lease condensate, which is subject to export restrictions. While there is no quality characteristic (i.e., API gravity) that defines lease condensate, increasing production volumes of condensate and condensate-like material is one aspect of the crude oil export debate. For additional information, see the text box below.

LEASE CONDENSATE: WHAT IS IT? IS IT CRUDE OIL?

Production of lease condensate, especially in the Eagle Ford formation in Texas, has emerged as a topic of debate in the context of U.S. crude oil exports. As the name implies, condensate is generally a gas underground. When it is produced along with oil and gas, it "condenses" into a liquid at atmospheric temperature and pressure. According to one source, the majority of Eagle Ford condensate is being produced from natural gas wells, not crude oil wells.[56] While "lease condensate" is included in the BIS crude oil definition, there is a potential contradiction within the definition. BIS defines crude oil as hydrocarbons that existed in liquid phase underground. However, condensate is generally in a gas phase underground and condenses to a liquid at atmospheric conditions. This apparent contradiction, along with other considerations, raises questions about the applicability of export restrictions to condensate. As a point of comparison, the Energy Information Administration defines condensate as follows:

> **Condensate (lease condensate):** Light liquid hydrocarbons recovered from lease separators or field facilities at associated and non-associated natural gas wells. Mostly pentanes [hydrocarbons with five carbon atoms] and heavier hydrocarbons. Normally enters the crude oil stream after production.[57]

There does not appear to be a standard quality characteristic—such as API gravity—used to classify what is and is not lease condensate. Additionally, there is limited information available that quantifies actual and expected volumes of condensate produced on an annual basis, because lease condensate is typically classified as crude oil for reporting purposes.

As a result, it can be difficult to accurately assess condensate production volumes when considering policy options that might allow this material to be exported. According to one estimate, lease condensate production in 2013 was approximately 1 million bbl/d and may reach 1.6 million bbl/d by 2018.[58]

Furthermore, the EIA definition of condensate is very similar to the definition of "natural gasoline," which is defined as being "equivalent to pentanes plus."[59] Natural gasoline is a product of gas processing facilities. Some market analysts have indicated that depending on the season—winter or summer—identical hydrocarbons can be classified as either natural gasoline, which can be exported without restriction, or condensate, which is subject to export restrictions.[60]

Additionally, the BIS crude oil definition states that crude oil hydrocarbons that have not passed through a distillation tower are subject to export restrictions. In order to comply with the regulation, investments are being made to install stand-alone condensate splitters—essentially a basic distillation tower—that separate the components (e.g., naphtha) of condensate. The resulting condensate components are eligible for export to international markets. As a result of the above considerations, some industry stakeholders have called for condensate to be removed from the BIS definition.

Actual and projected LTO production levels are affecting the refining and infrastructure segments in a variety of ways, and vice versa. How these segments might adjust to changing market conditions (i.e., increased LTO production) will depend on multiple economic variables and investment considerations.

U.S. Refinery Configurations[61]

As of October 2013, there were 115 oil refineries in the United States with a total operable capacity of 17.8 million barrels per day of crude oil throughput.[62] Each refinery has its own unique configuration that is generally designed to economically optimize the use of a certain crude oil blend and the production of oil products that will maximize profit margins. In the context of exporting crude oil, refineries located in the PetroleumAdministration for Defense District (PADD) 3 provide an illustration of some of the emerging complexities and economic decisions that are being considered as LTO production increases in the Gulf Coast area, and as Canadian and Midwest crudes are delivered to the region.[63]

There are 43 refineries located in PADD 3, with a total operable refining capacity of approximately 9.1 million barrels per day, the largest concentration of refining capacity in the country.[64] Nearly half of the refineries in PADD 3 are equipped with coking units (**Figure 3**), a refinery process that upgrades heavy residual material from a refinery's distillation unit and converts this material into higher-value products such as naphtha and distillate.[65] Adding a coking unit to a refinery is an expensive endeavor, with estimated costs in the $1 billion+ range. Generally, the decision to add coking capacity to a refinery is based on an expectation that the refinery will be able to purchase heavier crude oils that generally sell at a discount, and can yield certain oil products that are highly valued in domestic and international markets. Approximately 60% of PADD 3 refiners are considered coking refineries (**Figure 3**). Investments in coking capacity were made based on an expectation that price-discounted heavy crudes from Canada and Latin America would be increasingly available.

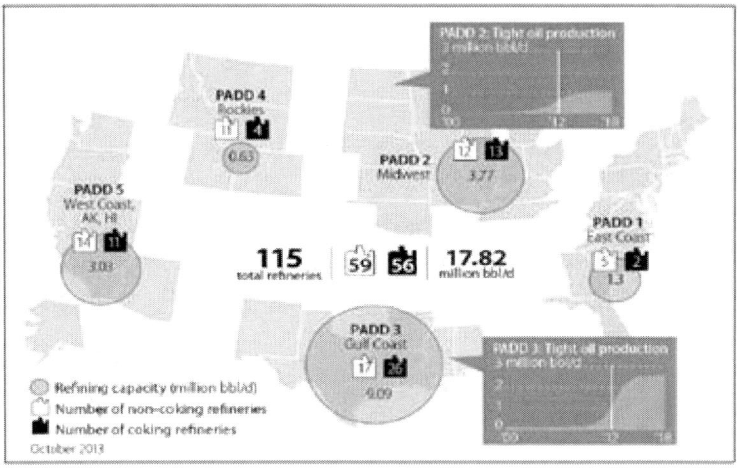

Source: Energy Information Administration, CRS.

Notes: Numbers may not sum due to rounding. PADD 2 tight oil production is for Bakken only. PADD 3 tight oil production reflects actual and expected crude oil production in both the Eagle Ford and Permian Basin formations. Tight oil production numbers are from EIA's 2014 Annual Energy Outlook reference case scenario.

Figure 3. Oil Refining Capacity and Coking Refinery Capacity by PADD.

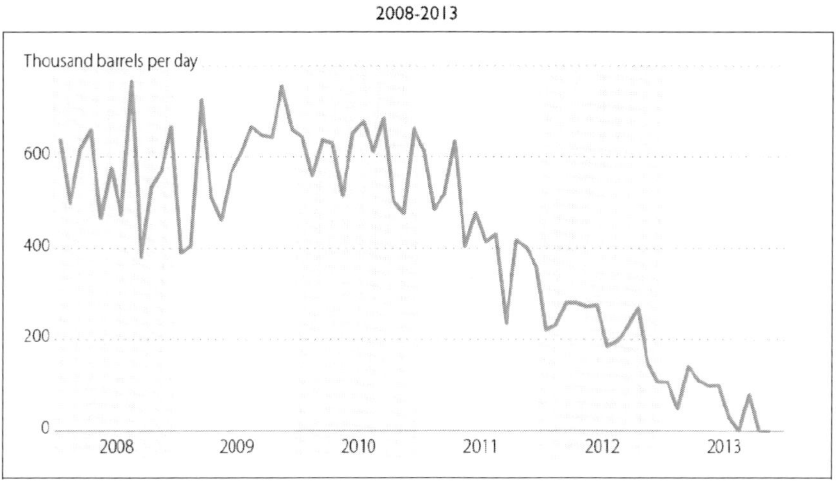

Source: CRS using data from the Energy Information Administration. See EIA website, *Petroleum & Other Liquids: Imports/Exports & Movements*, http://www.eia.gov/petroleum/data.cfm#imports, accessed January 28, 2014.

Figure 4. PADD 3 Light, Sweet Crude Oil Imports from Nigeria.

Increased production—both actual and forecasted—of LTO in PADD 3, primarily from the Eagle Ford and Permian Basin tight oil formations, may cause some refiners in this region to assess their optimal economic operating parameters. Each individual refiner will likely evaluate economic conditions—crude oil prices and product values—to determine if processing additional volumes of LTO is economically justified. While it may be challenging for PADD 3 refiners to process increasing volumes of LTO based on a refinery's current configuration, investments can be made to handle additional volumes of LTO. However, LTO price discounts, product values and volume commitments, investment requirements, and economic optimization for each individual refinery will dictate the additional volume of LTO that is ultimately absorbed. Whether such investments might actually be made is beyond the scope of this report.

In addition to making investments in refining equipment, reducing import volumes of light sweet crude into PADD 3 is one possible avenue for absorbing more domestically produced LTO, but some refiners may have already exhausted this option. Indications are that light sweet crude imports are approaching extremely low levels and there may be limited opportunities to further reduce light sweet imports—based on current refinery configurations—if U.S. LTO production continues to increase as projected. As an example, PADD 3 light sweet imports from Nigeria were at or near zero at the end of 2013 (**Figure 4**).

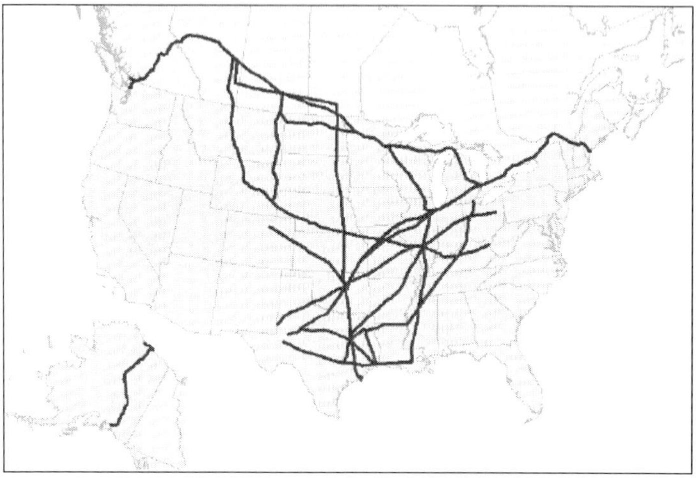

Source: CRS using data from Platts Quarter 4, 2013 dataset. Map created on February 6, 2014.

Notes: The figure above is a simplified illustration of the U.S. crude oil pipeline network. Many small and short distance pipelines are not included.

Figure 5. Major U.S. and Canadian Crude Oil Pipelines.

Additionally, some estimates project that total North American light crude oil imports may go to zero by the end of 2014.[66] Once total light crude imports are reduced to zero, refiners may begin evaluating options to reduce medium- and heavy-quality crude imports. However, foreign oil suppliers—notably Saudi Arabia and Venezuela—have ownership positions in some U.S. refinery assets. These countries could choose to continue providing oil, in some cases at discounts compared to available U.S. crudes, to their U.S. refineries in order to maintain presence in the U.S. oil market. Should countries elect this option, there may be limits to reducing crude oil imports. The ability of refiners to utilize more LTO is one consideration. However, transporting crude oil from production fields to refiners is another issue that can impact LTO price discounts and refining economics.

Infrastructure Challenges

One consideration for U.S. oil producers is the availability and cost of transportation infrastructure to deliver crude oil to refineries. Delivery infrastructure, and the cost associated with various transportation modes, can affect the value of oil that is produced in certain locations. LTO production growth in certain parts of the country is resulting in some constraints associated with moving crude oil to refiners.[67]

Crude oil is transported via pipeline, rail, marine vessel, and truck. Pipelines are the primary means of crude oil transportation in the United States. Generally, the U.S. crude oil pipeline network was originally designed to move crude oil and petroleum products generally northward from the Gulf Coast to Cushing, Oklahoma, and other destinations (See **Figure 5**). The geographic distribution of LTO production—currently concentrated in North Dakota and Texas— is constraining the existing U.S. pipeline delivery system, thereby creating market access challenges for some oil producers.

To address these challenges, the crude oil transportation network is evolving: (1) some pipelines are reversing oil flow direction,[68] (2) new pipelines are being developed,[69] (3) rail shipments are increasing to deliver LTO from North Dakota to the east and west coasts, as well as the Gulf Coast,[70] and (4) LTO waterborne shipments are also increasing. Waterborne shipments must comply with JonesAct requirements.[71] Transportation costs and constraints contribute to different oil values at various delivery points throughout the country. While infrastructure adjustments are occurring, it is unclear how much LTO volume these adjustments will ultimately accommodate. Depending on their location and the cost of transportation modes available, some oil producers may argue that allowing crude oil to be exported would serve to equalize prices by alleviating some of the infrastructure-related price discounts in the market. Infrastructure limitations and resulting price discounts will impact the volumes of oil produced as well as refiner decisions to utilize incremental LTO production.

Crude Oil Producer Prices

Ultimately, the objective of U.S. oil producers is to maximize the value, or selling price, of each barrel of oil produced. U.S. oil producers throughout the country receive different prices, which can be affected by oversupply in a certain region due to production levels, refinery demand, and/or infrastructure limitations. **Figure B-1** in **Appendix B** provides price history information for selected crude oil types. Allowing crude oil to be freely exported may have the result, all other things being equal, of reducing producer price discounts in some parts of the country, thereby equalizing the value of LTO to match global crude prices, adjusted for quality and yield characteristics and the cost of transportation. However, allowing crude oil prices to normalize may negatively impact certain refiners that are currently profitable due, in part, to regional crude oil price discounts.

For example, spot prices for Bakken LTO have experienced price discounts compared to the U.S. West Texas Intermediate (WTI) benchmark. EIA reports that Bakken discounts have been as high as $28 per barrel, but have since adjusted—a result of changes to the oil transportation network (see "Infrastructure Challenges" section above)—to lower levels as logistic constraints have been alleviated in the region.[72] Eagle Ford LTO in Texas has not experienced significant price discounts like those observed in the Bakken, likely due to its relatively closer proximity to refining customers and fewer transportation challenges. Eagle Ford condensate prices are more difficult to assess (see "Condensate" text box above). While official price information does not include a condensate category, some refiners do post prices for various crude types, including condensate. A February 2014 price bulletin shows an Eagle Ford condensate price discount of $6.50 per barrel, compared to Eagle Ford crude oil.[73] This discount suggests that condensate may be a less desirable feedstock for certain refineries.

As LTO production increases, transportation bottlenecks and limited refinery demand for LTO and condensate feedstock may put downward pressure on LTO producer prices. While refining and transportation adjustments will likely occur, lower prices may result in less oil production, depending on the severity of the price discount and the economics of specific oil production projects. Furthermore, the relationship between producer prices and refinery acquisition costs is dynamic. As transportation networks and refinery configurations adjust to a changing crude oil slate, prices should reflect bottlenecks and limitations that exist. Under constraint conditions, the price discounts needed to motivate system modifications, in combination with price levels needed to incentivize incremental oil production, are uncertain and can be difficult to estimate due to the integrated and dynamic nature of production, transportation, and refining. Such estimates are beyond the scope of this report.

CONSIDERATIONS FOR CONGRESS

Debate about U.S. crude oil exports is complex, dynamic, multidimensional, and includes many different stakeholder views. As a result, there are several issues that Congress may consider during future debate about crude oil exports. The following sections discuss some of these considerations.

Price Effects

According to the economic theory of international trade, opening markets to world trade tends to push the domestic price of the traded good toward the world price. Additionally, if the volume of products entering the world market is sufficiently large, the world price may also adjust to account for the new world supplies. Although the U.S. oil market has been open to world trade for many years, it has generally been in one direction. While large volumes of imported crude oil have helped to provide for the consumption of petroleum products, exports of crude oil have essentially been prohibited. The price of oil is determined on the world market, and any changes in demand and/or supply which might be expected to affect the price of oil must be set against world levels of market activity. As the United States considers whether to allow the export of domestic crude oil to the world market, price changes are likely to occur consistent with those suggested by international trade theory.

Crude Oil Prices

The price effects of allowing the export of crude oil from the United States to the world market are likely to be threefold. First, the domestic price of LTO, or other grades of exported oil, is likely to converge toward the world price. Second, the price of the U.S. reference crude grade— West Texas Intermediate (WTI)—is likely to adjust relative to world reference grade crude oils, notably Brent.[74] Third, the world price of oil is likely to adjust to reflect added U.S. supplies to the world total, all else being equal. See **Figure B-1** in **Appendix B** for price history information for selected crude oil types.

The actual magnitude of these price effects will be determined by the volume of crude exports from the United States that actually materialize. For example, should U.S. exports of LTO settle at about 500,000 barrels per day,[75] this would represent nearly one half of the total output from the Bakken field in 2013, 2.5% of total U.S. consumption, and 0.5% of world demand for oil.[76] As a result, the observed price effects on Bakken, and other price-discounted domestic crude oils might be expected to be relatively large, while the effects on U.S. reference prices and the world price of oil might well be smaller.

Shale based LTO, since its entry to the U.S. market, has sold at a discounted price relative to other domestic crude oils of similar quality. As described in this report, the location of the oil, the lack of infrastructure to move the oil to refineries, and the technological characteristics of U.S. refineries all contributed to the need of suppliers to discount the price to induce refiners to purchase available supplies. The EIA reported that since 2012 the price of Bakken crude oil has been discounted by as much as $28 per barrel compared to WTI.[77] While price discounts were less during most of the years 2012-2013, discounts were necessary to help cover the added cost of rail shipment of Bakken crude oil, which averages $10 to $15 per barrel nationwide. Rail shipment costs are as much as three times the cost of shipping oil by pipeline.[78]

Allowing the export of LTO would likely create additional demand for these crude oils that could cause the price to rise from discounted levels in the U.S. market to approach those earned by other light, sweet crudes in the world market. This would have the effect of reducing or eliminating the discount experienced in the U.S. market. Transportation infrastructure limitations would likely limit the quantities of exportable oil and add to its cost, but the potentially higher price earned by producers could help expand the industry. Investment in the fields might increase and with it oil production and related job creation.

Introduction of LTO exports might also affect the price spread between WTI and Brent crudes. This could happen as the result of two price effects. First, as domestic LTO becomes relatively less available on the domestic market, reflecting the quantities entering the world market, the price of WTI is likely to rise as the domestic market tightens. Second, the price of Brent has been especially high since the Libyan revolution, which led to reduced supplies of light, sweet crude oil to Europe. While the direction of change in both prices may be estimated based on market theory, the actual magnitude of the price change would likely depend on the quantity of U.S. crude oil exported. A reduction in the WTI-Brent price spread as a result of these factors would be favorable for oil production and producers in the United States, with somewhat higher product prices for some U.S. consumers. A reduction in the price of Brent would primarily benefit European consumers, although the benefits of lower prices could extend to the world market.

An increase in supply of LTO to the world market of, for example, 500,000 barrels per day, or 0.5% of world demand, would not be expected to have a large effect on world oil prices. A qualification to this observation is that the elasticities of both demand and supply in the world market are very low. As a result, changes in the quantities demanded or supplied on the market can have exaggerated effects on price. Among the effects of U.S. exports might be a reduced call on Organization of the Petroleum Exporting Countries (OPEC) crude oil and an increase in effective spare oil production capacity in the world market.

OPEC provides crude oil to fill the gap between world demand and the total production from all other, non-OPEC, oil producers. Nations tend to use domestic crude oil and the supplies available from close exporters before calling on OPEC producers for supply. If the call on OPEC producers is reduced, this amounts to an increase in spare capacity in the sense that supplies, if withdrawn from the market, could re-enter the market in the event of an unanticipated demand increase or a supply emergency. An increase in spare capacity might be expected to reduce the potential for price volatility in the oil market. The escalating prices of the summer of 2008 were associated with a period of high demand that strained available supply, which caused excess capacity to fall to low levels.

Product Prices

Changes in the prices of petroleum products directly affect consumer costs and behavior at the pump. According to EIA, 68% of the consumer's cost of gasoline and 57% of the consumer's cost of diesel fuel is directly attributable to the refiner's cost of crude oil. Therefore, changes in the price of crude oil are likely to result in proportional changes in the prices of petroleum products. This implies that the crude oil price effects analyzed in the previous section of this report will directly affect U.S. consumers.

The observed price discounts on Bakken crude largely, but not entirely, accrued to refiners supplying the Midwest and Rocky Mountain regions. A result of the availability of discounted crude oil may be that gasoline and other petroleum product prices were lower in those regions, compared to the national average. For example, during the period January 2012 through January 2014 Midwest gasoline prices were lower than national average gasoline prices during 21 of 24 months. As the price of local crude oil supplies rises to reflect convergence with the world price of oil, the benefit of these lower prices to regional consumers is likely to be reduced.

If world oil prices decline as a result of U.S. exports, this could result in somewhat lower petroleum product prices for U.S. consumers as refiners use a mixture of domestic and imported crude oils that are tied to the world price of oil. This could occur if the quantity weighted reduction in world prices more than offset the quantity weighted increase in regional domestic prices. Although a fall in world oil prices might be predicted, its magnitude may be small should the amount of U.S. crude oil exports be small relative to the world market.

By contributing to an increase in world spare capacity, U.S. exports could contribute to less volatile prices in the world oil market. Price stability, coming from less reaction to the numerous supply problems that plague the supply side of the market, could reduce market uncertainty, possibly bringing benefits to national and international energy planners.

Energy Security and Geopolitics

Although there has been some debate over U.S. crude oil exports, the effects of rising U.S. oil production have already been felt in international markets and on geopolitics. While increased oil production has allowed the United States to alter its geopolitical posture, the U.S. government has not used its oil production as leverage over other countries, and has been critical of countries that do.[79] Furthermore, the U.S. government does not directly control either oil production or the companies that do produce oil.

The rise in U.S. production has decreased the need for imports, improving the U.S. trade balance, and leaving more oil and spare production capacity on the world market. It has also contributed to an increase in refined petroleum product exports, an activity not prohibited by U.S. law. The change in perspective of the United States being a major oil importer to possibly an exporter has altered the United States'place in world energy. Countries that viewed the United States as a declining economic power now view it as having competitive advantages in new sectors related to petroleum. Some oil producing countries that viewed the United States as a market destination may now view it as a competitor.

If the United States changes its import/export position and potentially its rules regarding crude exports, the effects on geopolitics will differ depending upon how and when the changes occur in addition to the expected volume of exports. In the short term, as has already been raised, the United States may consider allowing more exports of crude oil to correct a possible market inefficiency due to refining capacity and crude oil specifications. In the medium term, whether U.S. laws will be changed to allow greater export of crude oil remains a key question. In the long term, if U.S. laws and regulations were changed to promote crude oil exports, how big of an exporter would the United States become remains the central question to the impact on geopolitics.

The U.S. posture towards sanctions against Iran, including by some Members of Congress, has become more stringent, in part because of the rise in U.S. oil production.[80] Additionally, the decline in U.S. imports has made the United States less reliant on certain OPEC countries, primarily Nigeria (see **Figure 4**).[81] OPEC, at least publicly, has "welcomed" the rise in U.S. oil production as stabilizing to the market.[82] Saudi Arabia, the world's largest crude oil exporter, has also indicated support for increased U.S. oil production as well as exports.[83] However, some analysts argue that the United States is shifting its interest (i.e., military presence) from key oil producing regions, like the Middle East, because of its newfound resources.[84] Additionally, other industry analysts speculate that Saudi Arabia may discount its crude oil and refined product exports to the United States in order to stay in the U.S. market for strategic reasons.

U.S. consumption of petroleum products was 18.49 million barrels per day in 2012 compared to the peak rate of 20.80 million barrels per day in 2005. In 2012, the United States produced 6.49 million barrels per day of crude oil and imported 8.53 million barrels per day with the difference between consumption and production plus imports being made up of non-crude oil inputs (i.e., natural gas liquids, biofuels, refinery gain) to the refining system. In 2005, the United States produced 5.18 million bbl/d and imported 10.13 million bbl/d. Over two-thirds of imports came from Canada, Saudi Arabia, Mexico, and Venezuela in 2012 and almost 60% in 2005.[85]

Canada and Mexico are considered to be reliable suppliers. SaudiArabia and Venezuela, both OPEC members, own extensive refining assets in the United States (Motiva and Citgo refineries respectively) and as a result might be expected to desire to maintain a presence in U.S. oil markets. Beyond these 4 countries, over 30 other countries supply the United States with crude oil, none at levels expected to be difficult to replace if emergency conditions might develop.

Should the United States remove barriers to crude oil exports, the amount of exports may not matter as much as the psychological impact. The view that the United States is committed to the global energy market may have the greatest effect. Even in the long run, most industry analysts do not project that the United States will produce more crude oil than it consumes (see **Figure 1**). Nevertheless, any additional barrels that the United States produces will dilute

OPEC's market share, assuming demand stays the same, and this may be viewed positively by most oil consuming countries.[86]

U.S. oil production is rising and is projected to rise, at least, through the beginning of the next decade. If the EIA reference case projections turn out correctly, the United States would likely resume its role as a growing importer of oil, assuming no other market changes. Changing geopolitical relationships because of the current situation may prove short lived if oil production does not continue to increase. Despite having a cartel supplier trying to manipulate prices, the oil market remains robust and competitive.[87] Being a part of this market has helped many countries, both producers and consumers. As an example, when the United States needed petroleum products after Hurricanes Katrina and Rita in 2005, European countries were able to supply them from their strategic reserves. Similarly, when Japan shuttered its nuclear reactors after the Fukushima tragedy in 2011, the energy market reacted by sending more natural gas, coal, and oil resources to the country in order to satisfy energy demands. Unlike earlier periods, the United States is now a participant in energy agreements through the International EnergyAgency to share the burden of supply disruptions on the world market. As part of its IEA membership, the United States maintains a Strategic Petroleum Reserve which can offset disruptions in imported supplies.

International Trade Policy

The potential exportation of U.S. crude oil may have implications for U.S. trade policy. The United States has undertaken certain obligations as a member of the World Trade Organization (WTO) and is a signatory to several regional and bilateral free trade agreements (FTAs).

As noted above, the United States licenses the export of crude oil under certain restrictive circumstances. The WTO generally discourages limitations on international trade such as import or export restraints. Underlying the WTO agreements are two basic principles: most-favored-nation (MFN) treatment and national treatment. MFN obligates a WTO member not to discriminate among the products of other member states. National treatment obligates a member not to treat another member's products as different from one's own. The General Agreement on Tariffs and Trade (GATT)Article XI, General ProhibitionAgainst Quantitative Restraints, states:

> No prohibition or restrictions other than duties, taxes or other charges made effective through quotas, import or export licenses or other measures, shall be instituted or maintained by any contracting party on the importation of any product of the territory of any other contracting party or on the exportation or sale for export of any product destined for the territory of any other contracting party.

However, some exceptions are available. Article XX provides a generalized exception that allows governments to restrict trade based on the conservation of exhaustible natural resources or the necessity to protect human health. However, these exceptions are subject to the provision that the objectives are not used as a disguised restriction on international trade or to arbitrarily discriminate between countries where the same conditions prevail. In this case, for example, restricting the export of crude oil may be dependent on a member's restriction of its own production.

The crude oil restriction may also be subject to the WTO's Agreement on Subsidies and Countervailing Measures (ASCM) if it, by limiting demand, drives down the price, thereby conferring a subsidy for domestic industry. This was one facet of a successful U.S. challenge to Chinese raw materials and rare earth export restrictions.

The United States is in negotiations on two multi-nation free trade agreements (FTAs): the Trans-Pacific Partnership (TPP) and the Transatlantic Trade and Investment Partnership (TTIP). TPP includes Australia, Brunei, Canada, Chile, Japan, Malaysia, Mexico, New Zealand, Peru, Singapore, and Vietnam. TTIP is a proposed agreement between the United States and the European Union. Countries in both of these negotiations may be interested in obtaining access to U.S. energy supplies. Both these agreements are directly relevant to exports of U.S. liquefied natural gas; according to statute it is in the national interest to approve LNG exports to FTA countries. There is no such exception for exports of crude oil; however, the EU reportedly has sought to put access to U.S. energy—including crude oil—on the agenda as a negotiating objective.

Environment

Potential environmental issues that could arise from the removal of crude oil export restrictions are dependent on the specific consequences that might ensue from removing such restrictions. However, these consequences, particularly the long-term effects, are uncertain.

A primary question for policy makers is the net effect on domestic oil production from removing the export restriction. As illustrated in **Figure 2**, EIA projects domestic production of LTO to increase dramatically in the near future. However, some observers have argued that the export restriction, coupled with current refinery configurations (discussed above), will effectively create a production ceiling for specific resources.[88] Assuming this is the case, the next question concerns magnitude: How much additional domestic production would occur if the crude oil export restriction is removed? Estimates for expected U.S. crude oil export volumes are uncertain and actual volumes will depend on multiple variables. As noted above in the "Price Effects" section, some estimate a potential excess of 500,000 bbl/d of light sweet crude oil by the 2015 to 2016 timeframe.

Assuming that lifting or modifying export restrictions would result in a substantial increase in domestic crude oil production—above what would otherwise occur—several environmental issues would likely receive some attention. These issues, discussed below, may include oil transportation, impacts related to oil extraction, and climate change.

Oil Transportation

A further increase in domestic crude oil production could amplify existing oil transportation concerns, which have received considerable attention. In particular, the current expansion of North American oil production has led to significant challenges in transporting crudes efficiently and safely using the nation's legacy pipeline infrastructure. In the face of continued uncertainty about the prospects for additional pipeline capacity, and as a quicker, more flexible alternative to new pipeline projects, crude oil producers are increasingly turning to rail as a means of transporting crude supplies to U.S. markets. According to EIA data, the volume of crude oil carried by rail increased by 423% between 2011 and 2012.[89]

While oil by rail has demonstrated benefits with respect to the efficient movement of oil from producing regions to market hubs, it has also raised significant concerns about transportation safety and potential impacts to the environment. The most recent data available indicate that railroads consistently spill less crude oil per ton-mile transported than other modes of land transportation.[90] Nonetheless, safety and environmental concerns have been underscored by a series of major accidents across North America involving crude oil transportation by rail.[91]

In addition, crude oil barge transportation may receive increased attention in light of the March 2014 oil spill in Galveston Bay, Texas.[92] On March 22,

2014, a container ship collided with an oil barge, releasing approximately 168,000 gallons of oil into the bay and closing the Port of Houston.

As with rail transport, crude oil transportation by barge has increased substantially in recent years (by 53% between 2011 and 2012).[93] However, the same dataset cited above indicates that tank vessels and barges consistently spill less crude oil per ton-mile transported than other modes of oil transportation.[94] Nonetheless, spills from barges and tankers often occur in locations that may be particularly vulnerable to oil contamination.

Oil Extraction

Based on the geology of LTO, hydraulic fracturing ("fracking") is often required to extract the resource. While the use of high-volume hydraulic fracturing has enabled the oil and gas industry to markedly increase domestic production,[95] questions have emerged regarding the potential impacts this process may have on both air quality and groundwater quality—particularly on private wells and drinking water supplies. The debate over the groundwater contamination risks associated with hydraulic fracturing has been fueled in part by the lack of scientific studies to assess the practice and related complaints.[96] These issues could receive additional attention if LTO extraction were to increase, due to a change in the U.S. crude oil export policy.

Climate Change

Some environmental groups want to keep the crude oil export restrictions in place for climate change reasons.[97] They argue that lifting the export restrictions would lead to increased crude oil development, which could potentially alter the "global carbon budget." The global carbon budget is a scientifically estimated maximum amount of net worldwide greenhouse gases that could be emitted without exceeding a proposed temperature target of 3.6°F above pre-industrial levels (a 2°C target). Some consider that such a temperature target could avoid the worst effects of greenhouse-gas induced climate change, and it has been agreed as a political consideration in international negotiations to address climate change under the United Nations Framework Convention on Climate Change. Assuming this estimation is correct, all countries' emissions (net of any sequestration or "sinks") would have to stay within the carbon budget to avoid exceeding the 2°C temperature cap.

However, the degree to which a change in crude oil export policy would impact the carbon budget is beyond the scope of this report. Moreover, there is no political agreement in the United States on a domestic carbon budget, on the appropriateness of the global 2°C target, or on the validity of any target.

POLICY OPTIONS

In light of the considerations discussed above, and as the debate about exporting crude oil evolves, various proposals might emerge that fall within a spectrum of policy options that Congress may choose to consider. At one end of the spectrum are calls to lift export restrictions entirely. At the other end are calls to keep, maintain, and possibly expand current export restrictions. Additionally, there are various proposals to ease crude oil export restrictions on a limited basis. The following sections examine some policy options that have been proposed or discussed.

Lift Existing Restrictions

One policy option that Congress may consider is to introduce legislation that amends EPCA. Legislation that modifies EPCA, and other export-limiting statutes, may be the most straightforward means of lifting crude oil export restrictions.[98] However, some Members of Congress have called on the executive branch to use its existing powers to either lift or ease current export restrictions.[99] For more information about executive branch powers related to crude oil export restrictions, see the text box below titled "Could the Executive Branch Amend or Eliminate Crude Oil Export Restrictions Absent Legislation?"

Should export restrictions be lifted entirely, U.S. oil producers would have access to global markets, domestic and international prices would likely converge to some degree, and domestic crude oil production may increase if the economics are justified. While this scenario might potentially benefit crude oil producers, some U.S. refineries may be negatively affected as a result of reducing regional crude oil price discounts. Additional crude oil production may also result in environmental concerns associated with expanded extraction, transport, and consumption. While unrestricted crude oil exports—all else being equal—may be expected to put downward pressure on global crude prices and domestic gasoline prices, whether actual prices will be lower is uncertain. Global crude oil prices are determined by a number of factors that are not controlled by U.S. policy makers (e.g., supply disruptions, Saudi

Arabia and OPEC decisions, and emerging demand from Asia). Ultimately, effects from crude oil exports on prices, the environment, and other considerations will be a function of the volume of crude oil that is produced and exported and will be further affected by the actions of other players in the global oil industry.

Maintain Current Restrictions

Congress could also do nothing, thereby maintaining the requirement for the President to limit U.S. crude oil exports. According to supporters of this position, maintaining crude oil export restrictions is warranted since the United States is, and will be, reliant on imports, and crude oil price discounts in the United States will be eliminated as domestic and global prices converge.[107]

Should existing export restrictions remain in place, there may be several potential outcomes to consider. LTO production is expected to continue growing in the short/medium term and existing refinery configurations may result in an oversupply of certain types of crude oil in specific locations (e.g., Texas). While refineries can adjust their processes to accommodate changing crude oil qualities, they will likely make the necessary capital investments to do so only if the economics are warranted. Lower, or discounted, LTO prices would be an economic consideration—along with the expected longevity of price discounts—for refiners when making capital investment decisions. Lower/discounted oil prices may result in less LTO production from certain fields.

However, the price discount needed to motivate refiners to make capital investments—and whether the price discount would be large enough to markedly reduce oil production—is uncertain. Nevertheless, maintaining current export restrictions may result in some oil producers receiving lower prices for oil produced.

Lower prices may result in less U.S. oil production, and therefore less economic development associated with oil production. However, discounted crude oil prices in certain areas may also enable some refineries to operate profitably, especially those in locations that benefit from price discounts.

Could the Executive BranchAmend or Eliminate Crude Oil Export Restrictions Absent Legislation?

Interest in reducing or eliminating existing restrictions on the export of crude oil has focused attention on the most expeditious legislative and administrative tools to accomplish this end. The most determinative means by which to accomplish this would arguably be the amendment or repeal of the current language in EPCA directing the President to "promulgate a rule prohibiting the export of crude oil" absent a determination that the export be consistent with the national interest and the purposes of EPCA.[100] However, the executive branch may have some options available to it even if Congress does not take this action.

First, BIS could amend the short supply control regulations restricting the export of crude oil. The statute mandates only that exemptions to the general prohibition be granted if an export is "consistent with the national interest and the purposes of [EPCA]."[101]

The restrictive language found at 15 C.F.R. §754.2(b)(2) could be amended to except additional types of exports from the general prohibition so long as BIS finds the change to be in the national interest and consistent with EPCA.[102] In order to change the pertinent regulations, BIS would have to follow the rulemaking procedures under the Administrative Procedure Act.[103]

Additionally, BIS could approve more applications to export crude oil pursuant to the "case by case" review authorized by 15 C.F.R. §754.2(b)(2).

Although the regulations do note that "generally" only certain kinds of narrowly tailored exports will be authorized, the regulations also note that "BIS will consider all applications for approval," suggesting the possibility that exports that do not fit the criteria outlined in that section may nevertheless be licensed by the agency.

If BIS finds that an increase in the types of exports of crude oil is in the national interest and consistent with EPCA, the agency is permitted to grant approval of those exports under the existing regulations that provide for case-by-case review.

However, it appears that BIS could not repeal the regulations entirely. As with all agencies, BIS cannot take any action beyond the scope of the statutory authority granted to it by Congress.[104]

Because EPCA states that the President, through BIS, "shall ... promulgate a rule prohibiting the export of crude oil ... produced in the United States,"[105]

BIS must have a rule in place that conforms with the statute—BIS would violate the statute if it simply repealed its regulations that impose a general prohibition on the export of crude oil. If BIS decided to repeal the regulation, any party aggrieved by the agency's decision would be permitted to challenge the action in court.[106]

Finally, as discussed above, the crude oil export restrictions are administered by BIS pursuant to a statute (EAA) that has expired, but continues to be effective due to annual executive orders renewing its provisions.

The President could reverse those directives via another executive order, or opt to not issue a new order when the current one expires. However, this could create a number of practical problems, as it would nullify federal authority to conduct all export control operations set forth in the EAA.

Also, while allowing the effectiveness of the EAA provisions to lapse would prevent administration of the BIS export license requirements, it would still leave in place the mandate of EPCA to restrict crude oil exports, a mandate that the Administration would be required to address.

Modify Restrictions

Between lifting oil export restrictions altogether and maintaining them in their current form are a variety of policy options that might be considered. Some examples of such policies might include the following:

- ***Exempt LTO from export restrictions:*** The increase in LTO production appears to be one of the underlying dynamics motivating exports. As a result, crude oil with a certain quality characteristic or crude oil that is produced in specific locations might be exempted from export restrictions.

The President has some powers to exempt certain crude oil exports if doing so is determined to be in the national interest. Exempting exports of certain types of crude from specific locations has occurred in the past. In 1992, then-President George H. W. Bush issued an executive order allowing 25,000 bbl/d of California heavy crude to be exported.

- ***Remove "lease condensate" from the BIS crude oil definition:*** As discussed in this report, lease condensate is an aspect of the crude oil export debate that is receiving attention due to increased production of extra-light hydrocarbons. Removing the term "lease condensate" from the crude oil definition may result in some of that material being exported, thereby addressing some of the apparent oversupply, and price discount, issues that may emerge in the Gulf of Mexico region. However, crafting a definition for lease condensate may present some challenges, as there is not an industry standard for this material.
- ***Allow crude oil exports for a limited period of time:*** EIA 2014 reference case LTO projections indicate that production may reach an upper limit by 2019 and then start to decline. While actual LTO production levels are uncertain, one policy option may be to allow crude oil exports only for a defined period of time—five years, for example—after which the domestic production and export situation could be reassessed.

There are a number of other options for modifying existing restrictions that might be considered.

Each option could impact the market and individual stakeholders in different ways. Congress may choose to study and analyze various considerations associated with efforts to modify crude export restrictions.

Appendix A. Crude Oil Export Applications Approved by BIS

Table A-1. ApprovedApplications for U.S. Crude Oil Exports by Destination, FY2008-FY2013

Export Destination	Oct. 2007-Sept. 2008			Oct. 2008-Sept. 2009			Oct. 2009-Sept. 2010		
	Applications (approved)	Value ($ millions)	Quantity* (thousand barrels)	Applications (approved)	Value ($ millions)	Quantity* (thousand barrels)	Applications (approved)	Value ($ millions)	Quantity* (thousand barrels)
Barbados				1	720	12,582			
Canada	29	50,181	466,048	30	31,185	544,946	39	38,339	497,032
China	1	a	b						
Italy	1	72	669	1	38	664			
Total	31	50,253	466,717	32	31,943	558,192	39	38,339	497,032
	Oct. 2010-Sept. 2011			Oct. 2011-Sept. 2012			Oct. 2012-Sept. 2013		
Canada	39	39,650	427,978	62	93,646	979,313	91	163,676	1,712,809
China	1	5,000	53,969	1	5,000	52,288	2	10,000	104,646
Costa Rica	1	44	475						
India	1	5,000	53,969	1	5,000	52,288			
Italy							2	3,120	32,650
Mexico							2	1,440	15,069
Panama	1	136	1,468				3	5,460	57,137
Singapore	1	5,000	53,969	1	5,000	52,288	1	500	5,232
South Korea	1	5,000	53,969	1	5,000	52,288	2	936	9,795
Total	45	59,830	645,798	66	113,646	1,188,465	103	185,132	1,937,338

Source: Information provided by BIS to congressional staff.

Notes: (*) Data is reported by BIS in dollar value. Quantity was derived using EIA monthly spot prices averaged for each fiscal year.

a. $1,000 b. Approximately 10 barrels

Appendix B. Crude Oil Price History

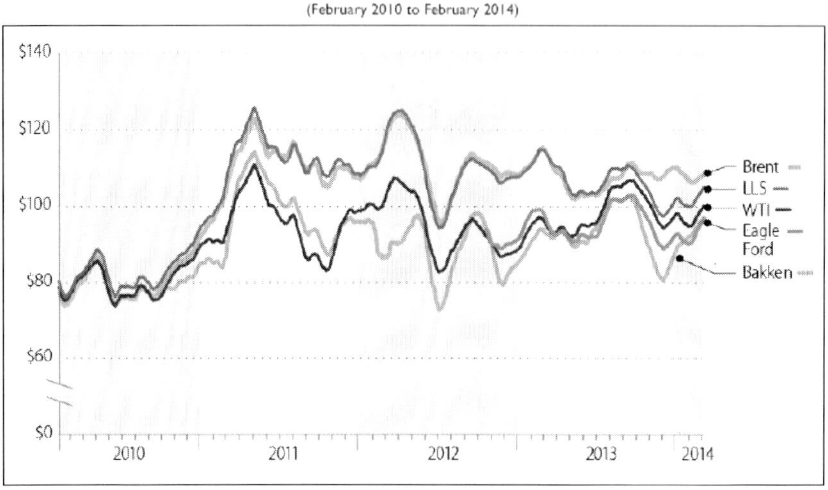

Source: Platts

Notes: LLS = Louisiana Light Sweet. CRS recognizes that WTI and Bakken price differentials, as reported in the figure above, are different than those referenced in the body of this report from EIA. Price information for Bakken in this figure reflects Clearbrook marketing point prices.

Figure B-1. Price History for Selected Crude Oil Types.

End Notes

[1] Energy Information Administration, *Annual Energy Outlook 2014 Early Release Overview*, December 16, 2013.

[2] See, e.g., Council on Foreign Relations, "Policy Innovation Memorandum No. 34: The Case for Allowing U.S. Crude Oil Exports," July 8, 2013.

[3] Energy Information Administration, *Annual Energy Outlook 2014 Early Release Overview*, December 16, 2013.

[4] Ibid.

[5] Naphtha is a refined or partially refined light hydrocarbon that is blended or mixed with other hydrocarbons to make motor gasoline or jet fuel. Naphtha can also be used as a solvent or petrochemical feedstock. For more information, see EIA glossary at http://www.eia.gov/tools/glossary/, accessed March 12, 2014.

[6] Energy Information Administration website, *Petroleum & Other Liquids: Imports/Exports & Movements*, http://www.eia.gov/petroleum/data.cfm#imports, accessed January 28, 2014.

[7] Senator Lisa Murkowski, "A Signal to the World: Renovating the Architecture of U.S. Energy Exports," January 7, 2014.

[8] Senator Robert Menendez, Letter to President Barack Obama, December 16, 2013.

[9] Senator Edward Markey, Letter to Ambassador Michael Froman, U.S. Trade Representative, December 3, 2013.
[10] Robert L. Bradley, *Oil, Gas, and Government: The U.S. Experience*, Cato Institute, 1996.
[11] Ibid.
[12] For additional information about events that led to the embargo, see Center for Strategic & International Studies, "The Arab Oil Embargo—40 Years Later," October 16, 2013.
[13] Federal government crude oil export regulations date back to as early as 1917. However, laws that currently restrict exports were enacted in the mid/late 1970's. For additional background on U.S. oil export regulation history, see Bradley, Robert L., *Oil, Gas, and Government: The U.S. Experience*, Cato Institute, 1996.
[14] For additional background about the Arab oil embargo, see Center for Strategic & International Studies, "The Arab Oil Embargo—40 Years Later," October 16, 2013.
[15] Energy Information Administration website, Petroleum & Other Liquids: Exports by Destination, http://www. eia.gov, accessed March 19, 2014.
[16] Ibid. Some non-U.S. crude oil was re-exported to China in 2013. Re-exports of non-commingled foreign crude oil are allowed under current export restrictions.
[17] U.S. Department of Commerce Bureau of Industry and Security, "Export Administration Regulations: Short Supply Controls," February 28, 2013.
[18] Crude oil slate refers to the blend of different crude oils a refinery might process to yield a desired set of petroleum products.
[19] For more information, see Energy Information Administration, "Crude oils have different quality characteristics," Today In Energy, July 16, 2012.
[20] P.L. 94-163.
[21] 42 U.S.C. §6212(b)(1).
[22] Ibid. at §6212(b)(2).
[23] 15 C.F.R. §754.2(a).
[24] Ibid. at §754.2(h).
[25] Ibid. at §754.2(i).
[26] 43 U.S.C. §1652; 15 C.F.R. §754.2(j).
[27] 15 C.F.R. §754.2(b)(1). For example, Canadian crude oil transported to the U.S. Gulf Coast via the controversial Keystone XL Pipeline, if it met the commingling requirement, would be eligible for export. For additional background and analysis of the Keystone XL Pipeline, see CRS Report R41668, *Keystone XL Pipeline Project: Key Issues*, by Paul W. Parfomak et al.
[28] Ibid. at §754.2(b)(2).
[29] Ibid.
[30] P.L. 96-72.
[31] For additional analysis of the EAA and federal export controls, see CRS Report R41916, *The U.S. Export Control System and the President's Reform Initiative*, by Ian F. Fergusson and Paul K. Kerr.
[32] P.L. 95-223.
[33] 50 U.S.C. §1701(a).
[34] *Executive Order 12322: Continuation of Export Control Regulations*, 66 Fed. Reg 44025 (August 22, 2001).
[35] *Continuation of the National Emergency With Respect to Export Control Regulations*, 78 Fed. Reg. 59107 (August 13, 2013).
[36] 30 U.S.C. §§181 *et seq.*
[37] 30 U.S.C. §185(s)(1).
[38] Ibid.
[39] Ibid.
[40] Memoranda of President: Exports of Alaskan North Slope (ANS) Crude Oil, 61 Fed. Reg 19,507 (May 2, 1996).
[41] 30 U.S.C. §185(u).
[42] Ibid.

[43] Ibid.
[44] 10 U.S.C. §7430(e).
[45] 43 U.S.C. §1354.
[46] For information and analysis regarding the scope of oil and natural gas exploration and production on the Outer Continental Shelf, *see* CRS Report RL33404, *Offshore Oil and Gas Development: Legal Framework*, by Adam Vann.
[47] 43 U.S.C. §1354(b).
[48] Ibid. at §1354(c). Note that similar legislative veto provisions elsewhere in the U.S. Code were declared unconstitutional in INS v. Chadha, 462 U.S. 919 (1983).
[49] For more information about SNAP-R, see https://www.bis.doc.gov/index.php/ licensing/ simplified-network-application-process-redesign-snap-r.
[50] Energy Information Administration, "Absorbing Increases in U.S. Crude Oil Production," *This Week in Petroleum*, May 1, 2013.
[51] EIA 2014 AEO.
[52] Ibid.
[53] Ibid.
[54] Turner, Mason & Company, "U.S. Crude Export Restrictions: Industry Responses and Impacts," February 28, 2014.
[55] Ibid.
[56] Personal communication with RBN Energy, LLC, February 7, 2014.
[57] Energy Information Administration online glossary, available at http://www.eia.gov/tools/ glossary/.
[58] RBN Energy, LLC, "Like a Box of Chocolates – The Condensate Dilemma," January 2014.
[59] Energy Information Administration glossary.
[60] RBN Energy LLC, "North American Oil and Gas Infrastructure: Shale Changes Everything," Presentation to the Center for Strategic and International Studies, November 14, 2013.
[61] For additional analysis of the U.S. refining industry, see CRS Report R41478, *The U.S. Oil Refining Industry: Background in Changing Markets and Fuel Policies*, by Anthony Andrews et al.
[62] Energy Information Administration, Refinery Utilization, and Capacity, http://www.eia.gov/ dnav/pet/ pet_pnp _ unc_dcu_nus_m.htm, accessed January 29, 2014.
[63] For additional information about U.S. PADDs, see Energy Information Administration, "PADD regions enable regional analysis of petroleum product supply and movements," February 7, 2012, available at http://www.eia.gov/ todayinenergy/detail. cfm?id=4890&src=email.
[64] EIA, "Refining and Utilization Capacity."
[65] For additional information about the coking process, see Energy Information Administration, "Coking is a refinery process that produces 19% of finished petroleum product exports," January 28, 2013, available at http://www.eia.gov/ todayinenergy/detail.cfm?id=9731.
[66] Raymond James Energy Group, "Still Bearish on Oil & Gas Prices But There is Light at the End of the Tunnel," February 12, 2014.
[67] For additional background about U.S. oil transportation infrastructure, see Energy Policy Research Foundation, *Pipelines, Trains, and Trucks: Moving Rising North American Oil Production to Market*, October, 21, 2013.
[68] One pipeline reversal example is the Seaway pipeline (between Cushing, OK and the Freeport, Texas area) reversal and expansion project. For more information see, Oil Daily, "Seaway Expansion Now Slated for Late Second Quarter," January 31, 2014.
[69] For example, Enbridge is in the process of developing the Sandpiper Project; a new pipeline that would transport Bakken crude oil from North Dakota to Wisconsin. For more information, see http://www.enbridge.com/ Sandpiper Project.
[70] For additional analysis, see CRS Report R43390, *U.S. Rail Transportation of Crude Oil: Background and Issues for Congress*, by John Frittelli et al.

[71] The Jones Act requires that vessels transporting cargo between two U.S. points be built in the United States, as well as crewed and at least 75% owned by U.S. citizens. For information about the growth in waterborne shipments, see Platts Oilgram Price Report, "US Jones Act fleet strains to meet demand," February 18, 2014.

[72] Energy Information Administration, "Bakken crude oil price differential to WTI narrows over last 14 months," Today in Energy, March 19, 2013.

[73] Flint Hills Resources (FHR) publishes price bulletins for various crude oil types. The $6.50 price difference mentioned above was derived from the FHR February 21, 2014 price bulletin by subtracting the difference between "Eagle Ford, crude oil less than 50 API" and "Eagle Ford Condensate, equal to or greater than 60 API." FHR price bulletins are available at, http://www.fhr.com/refining/bulletins.aspx.

[74] Brent crude oil is produced from the North Sea with similar qualities to WTI. It is generally used a benchmark for world oil prices.

[75] The export volume level of 500,000 bbl/d is used as an example only and was selected based on witness testimony and analyst presentations that suggest an oversupply of 500,000 bbl/d of condensate and light sweet crude oil in the 2015 to 2016 timeframe. For more information see, Amy Myers Jaffe, Testimony to the Senate Energy and Natural Resources Committee hearing titled "U.S. Crude Oil Exports: Opportunities and Challenges," January 30, 2014. See also, RBN Energy, LLC, Presentation to the Center for Strategic and International Studies titled "North American Oil and Gas Infrastructure: Shale Changes Everything," November 14, 2013.

[76] Export volumes will be determined by market forces and decisions by firms producing crude oil.

[77] Energy Information Administration, Today in Energy, March 19, 2013.

[78] Energy Information Administration, Today in Energy, July 26, 2012.

[79] Prior to the 1973 Arab oil embargo, world oil markets were controlled by U.S. and European companies. U.S. production played a swing role in matching supply and demand, and the Texas Railroad Commission dominated U.S. production. Concern with "energy security" is related to the reaction in the United States to the "oil shocks" of the 1970s when Americans first realized that the cost, and even availability, of gasoline could be interrupted for political reasons. Since the 1970s Presidents have sought, to one degree or another, to isolate the nation from the politics of world oil markets, to little effect.

[80] S. 965 was introduced in the first session of the 113th Congress calling for the expansion of U.S. oil production to displace all of Iran's exports on the world market.

[81] Nigerian imports to the United States are mainly light, sweet crude, which the United States is producing more of.

[82] Lananh Nguyen and Grant Smith, "OPEC Sees Shale as No Threat; Welcomes Output From Iran, Libya," *Bloomberg News*, January 27, 2014, online.

[83] Briefing by Saudi Arabia's Minister of Petroleum and Mineral Resources, Ali bin Ibrahim Al-Naimi, to congressional staff delegation, January 21, 2014.

[84] John Kemp, "America's energy revolution transforms international relations," *Reuters*, January 28, 2014, pp. http://in.reuters.com/article/2014/01/28/energy-diplomacy-idINL5N0L22YK20140128.

[85] EIA.

[86] Testimony by Amy Myers Jaffe, Executive Director of Energy and Sustainability, Graduate School of Management, Institute of Transportation Studies, University of California, Davis at the Senate Committee on Energy and Natural Resources' hearing, *U.S. Crude Oil Exports: Opportunities and Challenges*, January 30, 2014.

[87] OPEC tries to manipulate oil prices by controlling its production, but only Saudi Arabia maintains significant spare production capacity to adjust to immediate changes in market conditions, which is why it is referred to as the swing producer for oil. When production from other countries is disrupted Saudi Arabia may increase its production to maintain a target price, while it may cut production to make room for additional supplies from OPEC

and non-OPEC countries. However, Saudi Arabia has used its position for its own ends and contrary to OPEC's goals, most notably when it crashed prices in 1986.

[88] See Amy Myers Jaffe (Institute of Transportation Studies, University of California, Davis), Testimony before the Senate Committee on Energy and Natural Resources, January 30, 2014; and Maria van der Hoeven (International Energy Agency), "US must avoid shale boom turning to bust," *Financial Times*, February 2013.

[89] See EIA, Refinery Capacity Report, Table 9, June 2013. Note that this dataset indicates only the mode used for the last leg of such shipments. Some shipments may involve multiple modes, such as rail to barge.

[90] See CRS Report R43390, *U.S. Rail Transportation of Crude Oil: Background and Issues for Congress*, by John Frittelli et al. See also, CRS Report R43401, *Crude Oil Properties Relevant to Rail Transport Safety: In Brief*, by Anthony Andrews.

[91] Ibid.

[92] On March 22, 2014, a container ship collided with an oil barge, releasing approximately 168,000 gallons of oil, closing the Port of Houston. For more information, see U.S. Coast Guard updates at http://www.uscgnews.com and the National Oceanic and Atmospheric Administration website at http://response.restoration.noaa.gov/oil-and-chemical-spills/oil-spills/kirby-barge-oil-spill-houstontexas-city-ship-channel-port-bolivar.

[93] See EIA, Refinery Capacity Report, Table 9, June 2013.

[94] See CRS Report R43390, *U.S. Rail Transportation of Crude Oil: Background and Issues for Congress*, by John Frittelli et al.

[95] Hydraulic fracturing is used for oil and/or gas production in all 33 U.S. states where oil and natural gas production takes place.

[96] For further discussion, see CRS Report R41760, *Hydraulic Fracturing and Safe Drinking Water Act Regulatory Issues*, by Mary Tiemann and Adam Vann.

[97] Oil Change International, *Should It Stay or Should It Go? The Case Against U.S. Crude Oil Exports*, October 2013; and Paul Rauber, "Carbon States of America," Sierra Club Magazine, November/December 2013.

[98] EPCA is one law that restricts the export of crude oil. Other statutes include the Mineral Leasing Act, Outer Continental Shelf Lands Act, and the Naval Petroleum Reserves Production Act.

[99] U.S. Senator Lisa Murkowski, "A Signal to the World: Renovating the Architecture of U.S. Energy Exports," January 7, 2014.

[100] Repealing this language would not affect the restrictions on certain kinds of exports found in the MLA, OCSLA and NPRPA.

[101] 42 U.S.C. §6212(b)(1).

[102] In addition, any new rule or amendment to the existing rule would also have to be considered a reasonable interpretation of the statutory language. See, e.g., Motor Veh. Mfrs. Ass'n v. State Farm Ins., 463 U.S. 29 (1983).

[103] 5 U.S.C. §§551 *et seq.*

[104] See, e.g., Louisiana Public Service Comm'n v. FCC, 476 U.S. 355 (1986).

[105] 42 U.S.C. §6212(b)(1).

[106] 5 U.S.C. §§701, 702.

[107] During the 113th Congress, Senators Markey and Menendez sent multiple letters to the President and members of the Administration arguing that crude oil export restrictions should remain in place and should not be modified. Content and analysis contained in letters from Senators Markey and Mendez include (1) keeping U.S. crude oil in country and maintaining price discounts, December 16, 2013, (2) opposing attempts to use the World Trade Organization as a catalyst for changing U.S. export laws, December 3, 2013, and (3) Commerce Department authority limits and underlying export laws, January 30, 2014.

In: U.S. Crude Oil Exports
Editor: Michael Pope
ISBN: 978-1-63463-070-2

Chapter 2

TESTIMONY OF AMY MYERS JAFFE, EXECUTIVE DIRECTOR OF ENERGY AND SUSTAINABILITY, INSTITUTE OF TRANSPORTATION STUDIES, UNIVERSITY OF CALIFORNIA, DAVIS. HEARING ON "U.S. CRUDE OIL EXPORTS: OPPORTUNITIES AND CHALLENGES"*

The rapid growth of oil and natural gas production from unconventional shale resources in the United States has reopened debate on the question of U.S. oil and natural gas export policy. Foreign policy considerations should be central to the discussion of this issue. To date, the debate in the United States has focused mainly on domestic economic aspects and the possible benefits of actively promoting artificially low domestic prices through barriers to trade. Today, I will discuss the risks inherent the continued promotion of logistical bottlenecks, even in the face of rising domestic production. I will also elaborate on the national security and foreign policy benefits that the United States can reap by promoting an open energy trade policy that permits exports of natural gas, condensate, refined petroleum products and crude oil.

The United States has for many decades been the leading nation in championing open markets and free trade in energy. *Open trade and investment in energy is important to U.S. vital interests* for many reasons. First

* This is an edited, reformatted and augmented version of testimony presented January 30, 2014 before the Senate Committee on Energy and Natural Resources.

and foremost, artificial restrictions on energy flows can be a source of international conflict and, in fact, has been a factor contributing to armed conflict in modern history. Moreover, the United States, by virtue of both its superpower role and its position as the largest oil consuming country, has a direct interest in preventing energy supply from being used as a strategic weapon. Finally, barriers to foreign investment in energy resources in key countries generally contribute to supply constraints, leading to rises global prices and potentially harming economic growth in major oil consuming countries such as the United States and its key industrialized trading partners. For these three reasons, the United States should continue to actively support open markets and free trade in energy and to do so, it cannot restrict its own energy exports. By leading the charge on new energy technologies and exports, the United States now has the ability to fashion a global energy world more to its liking where petro-powers can no longer hold American drivers hostage or turn off the heat and lights to millions of consumers in the United States or allied countries to further geopolitical ends.

Beyond these core American values and interests, it is important for the United States to conduct a thoughtful debate and re-evaluation of current export policy to avoid creating market distortions that, while temporarily benefiting some consumers in particular U.S. regions, may create more questionable medium to longer-term trends that could turn out to be more damaging than helpful. Our history of energy policy is replete with such negative examples, such as President Nixon's inflation-targeted price controls on natural gas which ultimately caused a long lasting shortage of natural gas supply in the United States and a two-tiered system of oil pricing that ultimately, in practice, incentivized imports of foreign oil.

An evaluation of export policy needs to consider the following key variables:

1) Long term geopolitical considerations are likely more important to our nation than the expediency of any short term commercial gain to a particular set of vested industry interests.
2) Transportation and supply bottlenecks can create distortions that can become very costly in economic terms over time even if they bring some short term benefits to consumers.
3) The United States participates in international trade and thus, blocking exports of one or more particular commodities or manufactured products cannot "protect" U.S. consumers from international prices. Ultimately, the discussion of banning some exports and not others is a

question of who in the United States economy gets the profits from tapping the arbitrage of higher international prices. So for example, if gasoline prices are higher in the international market than in the United States, refiners will have a financial incentive to export gasoline until that arbitrage window closes. These U.S. gasoline exports will eventually produce the same boost in retail prices to U.S. consumers as crude oil exports.[1] That is because rising exports of U.S. gasoline to international markets will eventually erode profit margins for European, Asian and Latin American refiners, causing them to reduce their own refinery throughputs, lowering demand for crude oil and thereby weakening international crude oil price levels. In this way, rising U.S. crude oil production impacts global crude oil markets through displacement via U.S. refined product exports. Thus, it is not correct to say that the United States, by continuing to ban U.S. crude oil exports, can isolate American consumers from global prices. The often cited figures in Barclay's assessment of the financial savings resulting from the export ban oversimplifies the mechanisms and correlations of the interactions of U.S. and global gasoline pricing. Differences in elasticity of gasoline demand in the United States and Europe over different time periods (ie consumer responsiveness to price changes), differing refinery configurations and costs, weather trends, and local inventory levels all influence the differences between gasoline prices in the U.S. and Europe in 2008-2010 vs today, not just changes in the price of U.S. midcontinent crude oil relative to UK benchmark Brent crude.

4) The "tyranny of distance" for oil, refined products and natural gas trade flows will in most circumstances guarantee U.S. users a continuing energy cost advantage over foreign competitors even if export bans are lifted due to the generally lower cost of transportation within the United States compared to long distance, waterborne exports. This transportation cost advantage is, in many cases, of significant size and will ensure that U.S. energy prices are lower than those of countries that would buy U.S. oil and gas ex- ship. U.S. oil and gas short haul exports to Mexico and Canada are already protected by the NAFTA free trade agreement.
5) The best way to protect U.S. consumers from sudden price movements in gasoline, heating oil or natural gas from unexpected supply disruptions or weather related events is to ensure that adequate inventories are on hand in regional markets. To protect U.S.

consumers against volatility in fuel pricing due to shifting levels of global demand for refined petroleum product and/or natural gas exports, the United States should require U.S. producers and refiners to hold reasonable minimum inventories to guard against temporary domestic shortfalls of supply or seasonal volatility. Such minimum product inventory standards are already used successfully in Europe and Japan to enhance energy security and protect domestic markets in the event of an unusual event such as the Fukushima nuclear accident. In fact, the United States was able to weather Hurricane Rita and Katrina partly by borrowing gasoline from these mandated European minimum inventory stockpiles. As the United States shifts to a lower percentage of crude oil imports, it may want to consider holding a higher proportion of strategic stocks in the form of mandated commercially held stocks of refined products, rather than publicly held crude oil stores.

6) Crude oils and condensates from different geologic basins have different properties and are not fully fungible when it comes to refining them into usable fuels by various refineries. In particular, the light field condensate being produced in the United States from tight formations and shales require different forms of refinery distillation and other secondary processing than heavy oil production from offshore U.S. Gulf of Mexico, Canada, and Mexico. Top specialized analysts such as Alan Troner of Asia Pacific Consulting are forecasting that a large overhang of unusable condensate will emerge in the U.S. market by 2016 due to limitations on U.S. refiners' ability to process this particular quality of liquids. Relaxation of export rules for this class of associated liquids production would be desirable to maintain growth in production of natural gas and crude oil wells that also produce high levels of associated condensate. Asia Pacific Consulting estimates that as much as 500,000 b/d of the 3.5 million b/d to 4 million b/d of U.S. condensate production in the United States would not be easily absorbed into the U.S. refining and processing system by 2016 and might have to be simply shut-in until refiners can make investments to expand new units to handle such supplies, depriving the U.S. of export revenues and related trade and fiscal benefits (see appendix for more details).

GEOPOLITICAL BENEFITS

Energy trade can be used to *strengthen our ties to important allies and trading partners* and thereby enhance American power and influence. For example, U.S. LNG exports from the Gulf coast could be an important strategic back-up role to shaky Russian or Middle East gas supplies, for example, much the way the US served as an oil swing producer back in the 1960s, rendering an Arab oil boycott during the 1967 Arab-Israeli war infeasible. US Asian allies Japan and South Korea are seeking flexible US Gulf coast LNG contracts for reasons of economic and geopolitical leverage. Our ability to serve as a source for critical swing energy supplies enhances our importance to our energy trading partners in other geopolitical and economic spheres and *allows us to help our allies in times of market instability.*[2] It would, for example, constrain Russia's ability to use its energy supplier role as a wedge between the United States and its European allies.

As American shale production expands from natural gas to oil, the geopolitical benefits will mushroom both by *improving U.S. financial strength and by eliminating U.S. vulnerability to economic blackmail.* The upshot of shale oil will be to reverse the course of history and roll back the clock to pre-1973. Oil producing states will no longer be able to use the lever of a possible energy supply cut-off to America to pressure Washington to adjust its foreign policy. If domestic shale oil abundance someday more closely matches shale gas abundance and the US has no imports to replace, then we will have more discretion on when and how to use the Strategic Petroleum Reserve. In such circumstances, a President could consider using the SPR to either loan oil to other countries for geopolitical aims (for example, to *counter the economic blackmail of the "oil weapon"* against an allied country) or to provide extra oil into the market to head off attempts by coalitions of other energy producers to create artificial rises in global prices, should such oil price spikes start to cause financial or economic harm to the global economy.

In this regard, U.S. energy exports will *weaken some of our adversaries such as Iran and Russia.* US shale gas has already played a key role in weakening Russia's ability to wield an energy weapon over its European customers by displacement. By significantly reducing US requirements for imported liquefied natural gas (LNG), rising US shale gas production has increased alternative LNG supplies to Europe in the form of LNG displaced from the US market, *limiting some of Russia's power.* It has also already *curbed Iran's ability to tap energy diplomacy* as a means to strengthen its regional power or to buttress its nuclear aspirations by eliminating the need for

Iranian natural gas to potential importing customers by creating surpluses of alternative supplies. This remarkable development, by allowing the U.S. to impose tighter sanctions, has brought Iran to the negotiating table on limiting its nuclear program.

Energy exports also *improve our balance of trade*. The health of the US economy and fate of the US dollar come under pressure when rising oil prices raised our massive oil import bill, worsening the US trade deficit.[3] Such economic pressures are multiplied when we are forced by oil dependence to deepen our military commitments in the Middle East, thereby similarly adding to the US deficit. All this weakens the United States relative to China, which holds a large chunk of US indebtedness and free rides off expensive US naval activities to guarantee the free flow of oil from the Persian Gulf. Over time, shale development will reverse this strategic and economic disadvantage. As the years pass, it will be the Chinese economy that is more exposed than the United States to Middle East developments. Citibank estimates that rising domestic shale oil and gas production, by reducing oil imports and keeping "petro-dollars" inside the U.S. economy, will reduce the U.S. current account deficit by 1.2 to 2.4 percent of gross domestic product (GDP) from the current value of 3 percent of GDP. Energy exports would enhance this trend by adding gains to the balance of trade. As energy exports improve our global financial footing, it will not only *give us an upper hand with China*, which will still be highly dependent on foreign oil imports, but it could even allow the United States the luxury to regain its strong influence as a donor to global institutions such as the World Bank and United Nations, again enhancing our national power and influence.

Finally, energy exports are already an important *part of our free trade obligations* to important neighbors such as Mexico and Canada as well as more distant long-standing allies such as South Korea. U.S. law requires the U.S. Department of Energy (DOE) to review and approve any natural gas exports to countries with which the United States does not have a free trade agreement. Current rule making requires that exports to our free trade partner countries be approved expeditiously. For nations not covered by applicable free trade agreements, the review is supposed to lead to approval unless the project is determined to "not be consistent with the public interest." As a practical matter, the United States is already an exporter of domestic natural gas. The U.S. exported a total of 436.3 bcf of natural gas in the first quarter of 2013, mainly to Canada and Mexico. Canada has also been a major buyer of U.S. condensate. U.S. pipeline gas exports to Mexico are important to Mexico's economic health and to border relations and therefore it is unlikely the United States would ever consider cutting off Mexico's gas trade with us. South Korea now holds a Free Trade Agreement (FTA) with the United States. South Korea has indicated its desire to import U.S. Gulf coast LNG. Under normal economic conditions, it would not be in the U.S. economic and foreign policy interest to fail to honor our free trade obligations to South Korea while continuing to honor our obligations to Mexico. By extension, the United States, as an established exporter of natural gas, should not be turning away close allies like Japan and Europe. Since U.S. trade with Asia is important to our economic health, on balance it would not be in the U.S. interest to turn down Asian trading partners wanting to expand already massive trade to include natural gas, especially given that a preponderance of analysts have concluded that U.S. shale resources are large enough to minimize the pricing impact of LNG exports from the United States. This logic could also apply to refined petroleum products and condensates, which are already an important part of our current foreign trade.

Thus, I would argue that these many foreign policy considerations must be taken into account in any review on the question of the advisability of U.S. crude oil and condensate exports. We must consider all aspects of the implications of the energy export question on our national security and foreign policy interests. To focus only on the uncertain impact that exports might have on the U.S. industrial sector or gasoline prices in a specific region of the United States is foolhardy, given the complexity of interactive forces that will influence prices in the long run. Rather than second guessing price impacts which remain highly uncertain, we should widen the export debate to consider U.S. global priorities as well as domestic economic concerns.

In theory, the United States could behave like Russia and members of the Organization of Petroleum Exporting Countries (OPEC) and restrict hydrocarbon exports in general or to particular countries for political or nationalistic reasons. But we need to resist this temptation. Flows of U.S. oil and gas should follow profit incentives and market signals. The participation of American suppliers to the global market and foreign oil companies in the U.S. market extends the reach of U.S. anti-trust restrictions beyond our borders. It is true in general that foreign demand for American oil and gas can, all things being equal, put upward pressure on prices. But removing bottlenecks can smooth the functioning of markets, allowing arbitrage to promote flows to and from the most efficient geographic supply sources, eliminating localized volatility and easing sharp localized price movements during times of disruptions or unexpected events.

Efforts to engineer particular market responses on a local level can have unintended consequences. Greater U.S. cooperation on the global climate change agenda is of critical importance. Climate protection advocates worry that increased natural gas exports will lead to even greater use of natural gas instead of renewable sources. But bottlenecks preventing the free export of U.S. natural gas have, for example, led to the unintended consequences of increased exports of cheap displaced U.S. coal to Europe, unwittingly raising Europe's carbon emissions despite strong EU clean energy directives. Efforts to stop the construction of the Keystone XL Pipeline to ship Canadian oil sands has led to an increase in rail traffic of crude oil around the U.S., again with unintended environmental and safety consequences.

The more oil supplies there are and the more liquid those supplies are, the more the global market will mirror the competitive U.S. market. Supply bottlenecks are what aggravate price volatility to begin with, as any Bostonian can attest this time of year. New England's historical lack of local storage and limited pipeline deliverability has over the years produced sudden price climbs in cold winters. Had new pipelines like the Rex Express, which connects Colorado and Ohio, not been in place this year, recent winter price swings would be even higher and more prolonged. It is the same with the disruptions of light crude from Libya and elsewhere around the world this past year; but for U.S. products exports and the lower requirement for light crude imports to the United States, global crude price levels would be far higher.

As U.S. domestic production levels rise, the United States will have to think carefully about the kind of exporter it wants to be and how to promote the ideal level of free trade and energy investment wherever possible. The United States needs to consider the usefulness of past experiences when we counted on our European allies to provide us with badly needed gasoline from Europe's strategic stocks during our difficulties with the U.S. fuel manufacturing and distribution systems during Hurricane Rita and Katrina. And we need to think carefully about what our global economic and security obligations might be, should an oil supply crisis of major proportions emanate sooner rather than later out of the Middle East --both before, and even after, the U.S. gets closer to being energy self-sufficient. The mindset of husbanding resources out of fear of shortages has never served major producing countries like the United States well. In the crisis years of the 1970s, such hoarding behavior worsened the dislocations, not eased them. By contrast, in more recent years, we have fashioned an international emergency oil supply response system that protected the global economy in the aftermath of Saddam Hussein's invasion of Kuwait, and would be important should a similar or even worse kind of conflict were to arise again in an important oil producing area of the Middle East or West Africa. I am not saying that President Obama should turn open the spigot on willy-nilly, given the current instability in the Middle East. But clearly the circumstances of our energy situation is changing and we should not cling to historical policies because they are familiar and thereby politically comfortable. What is required is a thoughtful policy that is grounded in the realities of how energy markets operate and taking into account what is best for the economy as a whole, and not specific consumers or industries.

APPENDIX. FURTHER THOUGHTS ON MID-CONTINENT GASOLINE PRICES

The chart below, compiled with data from the U.S. Energy Information Administration (EIA) highlights that Midwest gasoline consumers are not, as has been reported in the media, reaping huge benefits from the crude oil discounts enjoyed by Midwest (PADD II) refiners compared to Gulf Coast (PADD III) refiners. The crude oil feedstock discounts enjoyed by refiners with access to mid-continent landlocked U.S. production (as illustrated by the blue line which shows the value difference in the crack spread between Midwest and Gulf coast refiners) did not lower the wholesale price of Midwest petroleum products compared to prices linked more closely to international markets, nor did they lower the retail prices of gasoline or diesel fuel prices in the Midwest markets served by PADD II refiners relative to the markets served by coastal refiners that do not enjoy these discounts. Since petroleum products are freely traded in a global market, U.S. petroleum product prices reflect international crude prices, not lower-priced domestic crude.

THE SPECIAL CIRCUMSTANCES OF U.S. CONDENSATE PRODUCTION

Liquid hydrocarbons suspended as particles in natural gas (under subterranean pressure and temperature) are called natural gas liquids or NGLs. Many tight oil and shale gas fields also produce NGLs, most commonly LPGs such as propane, butane, and iso-butane and condensate. Condensate typically remains liquid without special containment. It can be used as a petrochemical feedstock, a blending component, boiler feed, or as a diluent for the transport of heavy crude oil. It can also be processed directly in a splitter (special distillation tower design only for manufacture of light products) to produce lighter end refined products. Condensate is similar to ultra light, low sulfur crude oil and therefore is currently is being blended in with the rising tight oil production stream. For some previously marginal Midwest refineries that lacked sophisticated secondary refining equipment, the increase of light tight oil and condensate blend has been a godsend, raising profits by substituting away from scarce foreign imported feedstocks. But for the more sophisticated refineries on the U.S. Gulf coast, rising supplies of condensate produce greater challenges. These refineries need a sufficient volume of heavier fuel oil or heavy gasoil (VGO) as their feedstock to yield the optimum levels of gasoline, jet fuel and diesel production given the range of equipment in their facilities. Thus, there is a physical limit to how much condensate spiked crude oil they can use and still benefit from expensive coking units and to optimize the full scale of their distillation towers and facilities to produce the most valued combination of refined products. To some extent, refiners can blend some tight oil/condensate into heavier crude to add marginal volume use and tap the opportunity of the domestic production surge, but eventually to absorb all the condensate that is being produced, refineries will have to make large capital investment in new distillation tower capacity. Condensate's high naphtha yield reduces the working capacity of the tower. Valero is reconfiguring its existing tower at its Houston plant to be able to accommodate more condensate as is Marathon in Ohio and Kentucky facilities. Kinder Morgan is also commissioning a new splitting facility in Houston. But a lot of the rising U.S. condensate production is currently being sold to Canada for use as a diluent. By 2016-2017, the increase in condensate production is projected to exceed U.S. refiners and Canada's ability to absorb flows easily. As a result, the United States may need to relax restrictions for the export of field condensate or much of the incremental oil output from shale development will become increasingly physically unusable except outside the United States. In this case, lack of a clear export policy would lead to a reduction in further production increases of natural gas and tight oil.

End Notes

[1] In the case of gasoline exports, refining companies like Valero get a larger share of the profits. In the case of direct crude oil exports, oil exploration and production companies get the bigger piece of the pie.

[2] It is easy to imagine the expansion of American power if its natural gas companies could gear up to supply LNG to a European country cut off by Russia, such as happened in the winter of 2006. If the US can become an energy supplier of last resort, its geopolitical importance will rise significantly along with its diplomatic freedom of movement.

[3] For a detailed discussion of the link between the US dollar and oil prices, see Amy Myers Jaffe and Mahmoud El- Gamal, *Oil, Dollars, Debt and Crises: The Global Curse of Black Gold,* Cambridge, UK: Cambridge University Press, 2010

In: U.S. Crude Oil Exports
Editor: Michael Pope
ISBN: 978-1-63463-070-2

Chapter 3

STATEMENT OF HAROLD HAMM, CHAIRMAN AND CEO, CONTINENTAL RESOURCES, INC. HEARING ON "U.S. CRUDE OIL EXPORTS: OPPORTUNITIES AND CHALLENGES"*

Chairman Wyden, Ranking Member Murkowski and Members of the Committee, my name is Harold Hamm. I serve as Chairman and Chief Executive Officer of Continental Resources, an Oklahoma City-based independent oil and gas exploration and production company. It's an honor to address you today on the critical subject of crude oil exports. As Chairman of the Domestic Energy Producers Alliance and as CEO of the company that co-developed the first field ever drilled exclusively with horizontal drilling and the company that is the largest leaseholder and most active driller in the Bakken Play, I was in the unique position to be one of the first to see American energy independence on the horizon three years ago. And as technology continues to advance and new supplies of premium crude oil are discovered, today I see first- hand what's necessary to continue this American oil and gas renaissance and ultimately achieve energy independence for our country. I appreciate you inviting me to share my experience and insight with you here today.

In October 2011, DEPA put a stake in the ground and predicted American energy independence by 2020.[1] America's independent oil and gas producers

* This is an edited, reformatted and augmented version of a statement presented January 30, 2014 before the Senate Committee on Energy and Natural Resources.

have unlocked the technology and resources that make this a reality. As a result, we can today mark the recent 40th anniversary of the OPEC oil embargo by ending the era of oil scarcity in America and, along with it, ending the last of shortsighted regulations passed during that period.

The federal laws passed in the 1970s artificially controlled the supply, demand, and price of U.S. energy and brought about unintended consequences. For example, one law even banned the use of natural gas as a boiler fuel and mandated U.S. power plants switch to a less environmentally friendly alternative, coal.[2] Today America is still struggling to rectify the aftermath of this rash regulation.

In the years since the enactment of these laws, our elected officials have recognized our global energy industry has changed dramatically. Thankfully, in response to these changes, legislators have repealed or let expire nearly all post-embargo regulations save two: the Energy Policy and Conservation Act of 1975 and the Export Administration Act of 1979, which together essentially ban crude oil exports.

As the world has changed and other similar, post-embargo legislation has been phased out, the question has to be asked, "Why does the United States, a nation historically very supportive of free trade, continue to impose export barriers for domestic crude oil?" The fact is the supply and demand factors and "scarcity mentality" that originally led to the creation of these export restrictions in no way reflect the economic reality of the global energy marketplace of today.

We are entering a new era of energy abundance in America and the world. Heretofore, we have only been able to extract hydrocarbons from reservoir-quality rock, primarily through vertical wells. But through technological breakthroughs in precision horizontal drilling, we can develop resources previously thought to be unattainable. America now counts our natural gas supply in centuries, and experts including Raymond James,[3] Citi[4] and the International Energy Agency[5] all agree we will be energy independent in terms of crude oil within a decade or two. In comparison, this offsets a 2005 high of 60% crude oil imports.

This phenomenon was brought about by a group of independent American producers and missed by the general consensus of the industry. The American oil and gas renaissance was in complete contrast to the popular belief that the United States was running out of oil and gas at the turn of the 21st century. In fact, under expectations of a far different domestic production outlook only a decade ago, the U.S. refining industry invested many tens of billions of dollars to retool refineries to process heavy, high-sulfur bitumen and tar sands from South America, Canada and Saudi Arabia.

Not only has horizontal drilling increased America's supply of crude oil, but also it has improved the quality. Primarily the oil produced through horizontal drilling is light, tight, low-sulfur crude, making it the best quality in the world. It's environmentally friendly, it promotes jobs, it's fueling a manufacturing and petrochemical industry comeback in America, and we need to make sure we don't disadvantage this high quality oil with refining capacity, wherever it may be located in the world.

The popular belief is that we're not exporting petroleum. Nothing could be further from the truth. Major oil companies are exporting refined petroleum products like gasoline and diesel with no limitations.[6] Why shouldn't independent producers be allowed to do the same? Are we to be their subjugate milk cows, just like being able to export flour, but not wheat? No one will go for that.

Over the years, some have argued granting U.S. crude oil producers free access to world markets would drive up the cost of gasoline and other petroleum products for American consumers. The opposite is actually true. By imposing trade restrictions on a single segment of the energy industry, namely domestically produced crude, our government is arbitrarily subsidizing some U.S. refineries – many of which are foreign-owned – by giving them the ability to source American oil at prices well below the world market price, while at the same time giving them the "green light" to sell petroleum products into higher-priced international markets.

Energy independence is working – U.S. gasoline and diesel prices are down 20%. But America's oil and gas renaissance is in jeopardy. These outdated crude export restrictions have prevented domestic oil exploration and production from achieving its full potential – slowing potential job growth, restricting supply, and negatively affecting global refined product balances, which sends the wrong message to our trading partners around the world. Many refineries overseas designed to only process light, sweet crude similar to U.S. grades find it difficult to compete profitably with U.S. refiners with access to domestic crude at artificially low prices, forcing many to close and thereby reducing supplies of refined products on the global market.[7] This effectively raises prices for consumers in the U.S. and all around the world. Many refineries in the Caribbean, Europe, India and South America are closing or operating at sub-optimal levels as they cannot compete with U.S. refiners running on discounted domestic crude oil. And, when supplies of gasoline and diesel fuel are restricted in the global market, the global demand for U.S. gasoline and diesel increases, thereby driving up the price U.S. consumers must pay at the pump.

The true benefit to the American consumer will be competition for the refining of gasoline. Indeed, crude oil is no different than any other commodity, product, or service demanded by consumers. Lower prices are only brought about by increased supply, greater competition amongst sellers, weaker demand, or improved efficiency in the manufacturing and distribution process. When governments attempt to legislate lower prices through regulations, no matter how well-meaning the laws may be when introduced, market distortions and unintended consequences inevitably result; supply and competition among producers is rendered short of potential, and the consumer ends up paying higher prices at the gas pump and in their monthly energy bills.

America is at a crossroads. Do we cap oil production or allow exports? Lifting export restrictions will strengthen our domestic oil industry, a critical component of our economy whose impact reaches far beyond the American consumer. At a time when unemployment sits at nearly 7% and, more importantly, U.S. labor force participation has fallen to just 63%,[8] the energy sector has added jobs for millions of Americans – both directly and indirectly through energy service and equipment companies. It has also served as a job multiplier for our nation's growing chemical and manufacturing industries. To this point, a recent IHS[9] report issued in September 2013 on unconventional oil and gas – or oil and gas produced by horizontal drilling – found that:

- Employment attributed to unconventional oil and gas and petrochemical activity currently supports more than 2.1 million jobs. IHS projects it to grow to 3.3 million jobs by 2020 and 3.9 million jobs by 2025.
- In 2012, the unconventional oil and gas and petrochemical industries contributed nearly $284 billion to GDP. IHS projects this to grow to $468 billion in 2020 and $533 billion by 2025.
- Unconventional energy increased U.S. household disposable income by $1,200 in 2012. IHS projects the contribution to increase to $2,000 per household in 2015 and $3,500 per household in 2025.
- Unconventional energy activity and employment contributed more than $74 billion in government revenues in 2012 and is projected to increase to $138 billion per year in 2025.

By supporting the export of domestically produced crude, U.S. lawmakers can add to these totals in the form of increased jobs, GDP and tax revenues.

Beyond its economic benefits, supporting domestic oil production is vital for our national security. Indeed, the growth in domestic oil production over the past several years has contributed to a significant drop in U.S. reliance on imported oil.[10] But national security and oil exports are not mutually exclusive; in fact, they go hand-in-hand. The authorization of oil exports promotes investment in additional energy resource and infrastructure development at home, enabling our nation to better control its own destiny.

But energy independence doesn't mean being isolationist. As we've seen in Cuba, Venezuela and North Korea, closed societies don't work. Energy independence means energy security. It means a chance for America to step back into a global leadership role by creating a world of balanced interdependency as opposed to dysfunctional interdependency. And it means no one can choke off supply, turn on the tap, or otherwise distort the market.

In conclusion, the world has drastically changed since the OPEC oil embargo and reactionary enactment of federal regulations in the 1970s. Even then the ban was symbolic, as we had no oil to export. Americans and consumers of all nations would benefit from the immediate lifting of restrictions that inhibit the export of crude oil produced in the U.S. The net result of taking this timely action would be:

1. Lowering fuel costs to American consumers and businesses by matching light, tight, low- sulfur domestic oil with refining capacity designed to efficiently process this type of premium quality crude.
2. Promoting job growth in the domestic energy sector by encouraging tight oil production.
3. Raising tax revenue at the local, state and federal level through GDP growth.
4. Advancing America's march to energy independence.

End Notes

[1] Stephen Moore, "How North Dakota Became Saudi Arabia," Wall Street Journal (October 1, 2011)

[2] Powerplant and Industrial Fuel Use Act of 1978 (Repealed in 1987) http://www.eia.gov/oil_gas/natural_gas/analysis_publications/ngmajorleg/repeal.html

[3] Raymond James "Yes, Mr. President, We Believe We Can Drill Our Way Out of This Problem" April 2, 2012, Accessed January 27, 2014.

[4] Citi GPS "Energy 2020 North America, the New Middle East?" March 20, 2012, Accessed January 27, 2014.

[5] International Energy Agency "World Energy Outlook 2013" November 12, 2012, Accessed January 27, 2014.

[6] Exports of petroleum products have nearly quadrupled from 870 thousand bpd in 2006 to nearly 3.6 million bpd in 2014, making the U.S. a net exporter of finished products http://www.eia.gov/dnav/pet/pet_move_wkly_dc_NUS-Z00_mbblpd_w.htm

[7] Valero Investor Presentation November 12, 2013 http://www.valero.com/InvestorRelations/Pages/EventsPresentations.aspx, Accessed January 27, 2014.

[8] Bureau of Labor Statistics. http://data.bls.gov/timeseries/LNS11300000. As of December 2013.

[9] IHS "U.S. Unconventional Oil and Gas Revolution to Increase Disposable Income by More than $2,700 per Household and Boost U.S. Trade Position by More than $164 billion in 2020, New IHS Study Says," September 4, 2013. http://press.ihs.com/press-release/economics/us-unconventional-oil-and-gas-revolution-increase- disposable-income-more-270. Accessed September 24, 2013.

[10] Bureau of Economic Analysis, "U.S. Trade in Goods (IDS-0182)." Accessed July 12, 2013.

In: U.S. Crude Oil Exports
Editor: Michael Pope
ISBN: 978-1-63463-070-2

Chapter 4

TESTIMONY OF GRAEME BURNETT, SENIOR VICE PRESIDENT, DELTA AIR LINES. HEARING ON "U.S. CRUDE OIL EXPORTS: OPPORTUNITIES AND CHALLENGES"*

Good morning. Chairman Wyden, Ranking Member Murkowski, and Members of the Committee: Thank you for inviting me to testify before you today.

My name is Graeme Burnett. I am the Senior Vice President for Fuel Optimization at Delta Air Lines. In this position I manage Delta's jet fuel supply as well as serve as Chairman of the Board of Monroe Energy, the company that owns and operates Delta's refinery in Trainer, Pennsylvania. I have over 30 years experience in the petrochemical and refining sectors of the energy industry and, before coming to Delta, I worked in various capacities in Texas and across the globe for one of the top five oil companies.

Delta Air Lines is the largest non-military user of jet fuel in the world and, like all airlines, we participate in oil markets on a daily basis. Jet fuel after all is our largest expense. It contributes to the price of an airplane ticket, influences the types of aircraft we purchase, and helps determine whether we serve certain routes. Because of all this, we are uniquely situated – *both* as an end user of crude oil *and* as a refiner – to comment on the crude oil export ban and the current debate over whether to lift it. We believe strongly that the ban

* This is an edited, reformatted and augmented version of testimony presented January 30, 2014 before the Senate Committee on Energy and Natural Resources.

on U.S. crude oil exports is good policy. It is good for American consumers. And it is good for the airline industry and our passengers.

As we all know, the ban dates back to the 1973 oil embargo. With gas prices then soaring, Congress established a crude oil export ban to limit our nation's reliance on foreign oil and minimize the impact of volatile global oil markets on domestic gas prices.

While U.S. oil imports did drop in the 1970s and early 1980s, the ban did not– as critics will point out – insulate the country from foreign oil. In the years after the ban was created, this country remained vulnerable to volatility in oil markets and the price of a U.S barrel of crude – known in the industry as West Texas Intermediate or WTI – tracked the price of a barrel of crude that traded on the global markets.

All that changed a just a few years ago. Beginning in 2011, when the country began to feel the impact of the domestic shale oil boom, a barrel of U.S. produced crude became cheaper than a barrel of crude trading on the global markets. *See* Attachment 1. And today the going price for a barrel of U.S. crude is $96. That's about $11 less than a barrel sold in Europe.

This price differential can be easily explained. The U.S. crude market is a competitive one with price determined by supply and demand. Once the U.S. domestic market incorporated the increased supply of crude from places like North Dakota's Bakken formation, the price of a domestic barrel of oil came down. In contrast, the global market is influenced by an oligopoly where OPEC countries control production in order to set prices.

If we lift the export ban we would in essence be allowing the transport of crude out of a competitive market in this country and into a less competitive global one controlled by a few oil-producing states. The results would be easy to predict: U.S. crude would flow out of this country and onto the world market. OPEC would reduce supply to maintain high global prices. The United States' use of homegrown oil would diminish and prices here at home would rise to match the higher global price for a barrel of crude. As one commentator put it, allowing for the *export* of homegrown U.S. crude would do nothing more than *import* higher OPEC prices into the U.S. market.

It's clear who gains from this scenario: The oil exploration and production companies, many of which are foreign owned. With all the crude coming out of North Dakota, Wyoming, Texas, Pennsylvania and other states helping to push prices down, these companies want to lift the ban and sell U.S. crude on the global market at higher prices largely determined by OPEC. And it's equally apparent who would lose: The American consumer, who would pay more for gasoline, more for heating oil and more for the price of an airline ticket. In fact, according to Barclays PLC, lifting the export ban would stop the decline in U.S. crude prices and cost American motorists as much as $10 billion a year in higher prices at the pump.

Our country's refinery workers also stand to lose from lifting export limits. Some recent history can help explain why. Before the shale oil boom, there was too much capacity in refineries in the Northeast and along the Gulf Coast and many were closing. In fact, Delta purchased its Pennsylvania refinery in 2012 from ConocoPhillips after that facility had been closed for nearly one year.

The shale oil revolution breathed new life into these refineries and created jobs for thousands of refinery workers. By lifting the export ban and sending our crude overseas, we would reverse that trend. Refineries in Europe – where there is currently excess refining capacity – would be more than happy to refine our oil using European workers to do so. Put simply, lifting the ban will benefit European refinery workers at the expense of thousands of American jobs.

Furthermore, in thinking about the merits of the export ban, we should consider one of its goals: To help this country achieve energy independence; and by "independence," I mean the ability to meet our energy needs from sources within North America.

This country has benefited tremendously from increased domestic energy production in recent years. The shale boom and advances in production and extraction technology have helped us create jobs and reduce our dependence on foreign oil – and foreign regimes. Notwithstanding the upswing in domestic production, this country still imports around 33% of its daily crude oil needs from outside of North America. That's why exporting U.S. crude makes little sense. If we allow for the export of U.S. crude, we'll have to import more oil from overseas and subject ourselves, once again, to an increasing degree of price volatility and higher global prices.

In sum, the export ban works. It may have taken a bit longer than we anticipated in the 1970s, but we're now seeing its benefits: lower prices for crude in this country compared to global markets and an increase in homegrown energy. The ban may be unnecessary at some point in the future. But we still have a long way to go to protect against oil market volatility and achieve true energy independence. That's why - and I'll close with a sport's metaphor here - lifting the ban now would be like ending the game after the first quarter.

Thank you Mr. Chairman. I look forward to answering the questions that you and other Members of this Committee may have.

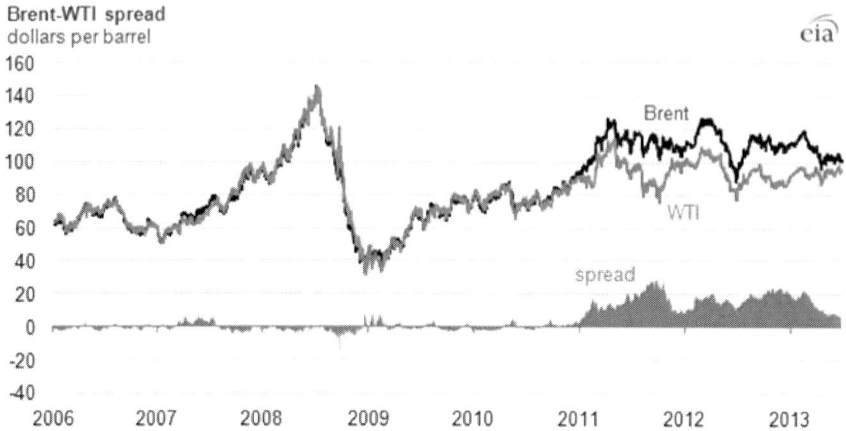

[i]Source: U.S. Energy Information Administration

Attachment 1.

In: U.S. Crude Oil Exports
Editor: Michael Pope
ISBN: 978-1-63463-070-2

Chapter 5

TESTIMONY OF DANIEL J. WEISS, SENIOR FELLOW AND DIRECTOR OF CLIMATE STRATEGY, CENTER FOR AMERICAN PROGRESS. HEARING ON "U.S. CRUDE OIL EXPORTS: OPPORTUNITIES AND CHALLENGES"*

Chairman Wyden, Ranking Member Murkowski, thank you for the opportunity to testify about whether to lift the crude oil export ban.

Since 2008, the United States produced more and used less oil due to advances in drilling technology and more efficient vehicles. This reduced oil imports and lowered our vulnerability to a foreign oil supply disruption that could cause a gasoline price spike. However, the Energy Information Administration predicts that the growth in oil production will peak in 2019, and domestic production will slowly decline after that.

Lifting the ban on crude oil exports could squander this new energy security and price stability. To maintain these benefits, we urge you to defend the domestic crude oil export ban.

After the 1973 Arab oil embargo, Congress enacted the Energy Policy and Conservation Act, which banned nearly all exports of domestically produced crude oil to keep this precious commodity at home and insulate drivers from price shocks.[1] At the time of the ban, the U.S. produced 64 percent of its oil

* This is an edited, reformatted and augmented version of testimony presented January 30, 2014 before the Senate Committee on Energy and Natural Resources.

and liquid fuels, while importing only 36 percent.[2] In 2013, we produced and imported nearly the same proportions of petroleum.

The only real-world experience of lifting an oil export prohibition occurred following the 1996 removal of a ban on Alaska oil exports.[3] During the ban, much Alaskan oil was shipped to the West Coast. A Congressional Research Service analysis found that lifting the oil ban exacerbated the existing price differential between West Coast and national gasoline.

> In 1995, West Coast pump prices [were] only 5 cents per gallon above the national average. But by 1999 West Coast gasoline was 15 cents per gallon higher. When crude exports stopped in 2000, the average [difference]...was 12 cents; it [later] narrowed further to 7 cents. ... When Alaskan oil exports ceased, the gasoline price differential between the West Coast and the national average did decline.[4]

This experience suggests that lifting the nationwide crude oil export ban could similarly raise gasoline prices. Barclays Plc. predicts that lifting the export ban could increase total spending on motor vehicle fuel by $10 billion a year.[5] Sandy Fielden, director of energy analytics at RBN Energy, told *Bloomberg* that if there are more oil exports "The most obvious thing that's going to happen is that crude prices will go up and so will gasoline."[6]

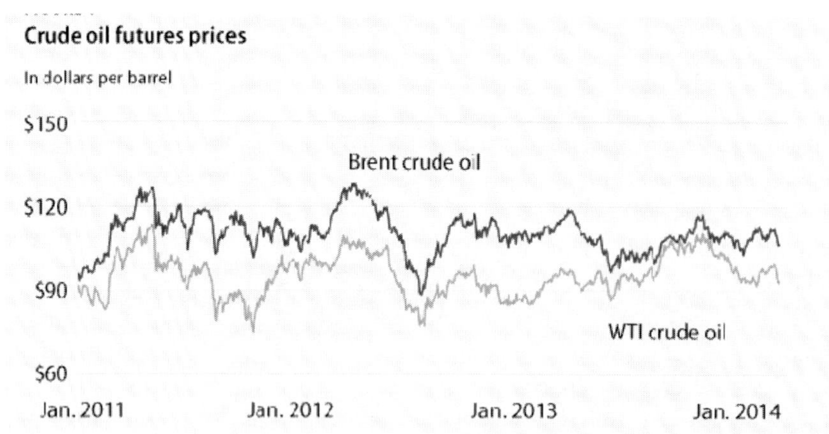

Source: Energy Information Administration, "Petroleum & Other Liquids: Spot Prices," available at http://www.eia.gov/dnav/pet/pet_pri_spt_s1_d.htm (last accessed January 2014).

If the ban is lifted, oil companies could sell some of their oil at the higher world market price, which the Energy Information Administration projects will average $9 per barrel more in 2014 for some domestic oil.[7]

The Energy Information Administration predicts that in 2014 the U.S. will consume 5 million barrels per day (mbd) of oil and liquids more than we produce. This gap between demand and supply will continue at least through 2040, ultimately growing by 13 percent. Domestic oil sold overseas must be replaced by more expensive imported oil. This higher price could be reflected in higher gasoline prices.

U.S. petroleum and other liquid fuels supply, consumption, and net imports

In millions of barrels per day

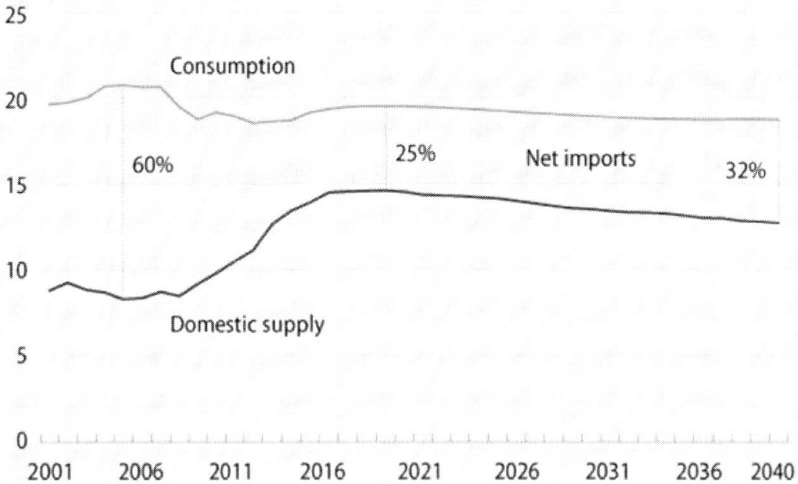

Source: Energy Information Administration, AEO2014 Early Release Overview (U.S. Department of Energy, 2014), available at http://www.eia.gov/forecasts/aeo/er/early_production.cfm?src=Petroleum-b2.

The U.S. imports more oil from the Organization of Petroleum Exporting Countries (OPEC) than from any other single source. OPEC oil is very vulnerable to supply disruptions.[8] EIA found that interruptions

> May occur frequently …for a variety of reasons, including conflicts [and] natural disasters … Total outages among the Organization of the Petroleum Exporting Countries (OPEC) producers recently rose to historically high levels.[9]

A commission of retired senior U.S. military officers recently noted that “No matter how close the country comes to oil self-sufficiency, volatility in the global oil market will remain a serious concern.”[10]

Oil produced in the United States is significantly less vulnerable to supply disruptions and therefore provides more energy security.

There is little benefit to Americans from lifting the ban, particularly since oil companies are already making huge profits even with it. The five largest oil companies – BP, Chevron, ConocoPhillips, ExxonMobil, and Shell – made a combined total profit of $1 trillion over the last decade, based on their quarterly financial reports.[11]

In 2013, the United States exported an average of nearly 1.5 mbd of diesel fuel and finished motor gasoline.[12] The sale of finished products enables American workers to provide added value to the crude oil. AFL-CIO President Richard Trumka opposes lifting the oil export ban because he believes that American workers should make crude oil into refined products here, rather than export it and refine it overseas.[13]

Our transportation system is almost entirely powered by oil and liquid fuels.[14] Since we continue to import one-third of our oil, American families, the economy, and our energy security remain vulnerable to sudden supply disruptions and price spikes. We must invest in alternative, non-petroleum transportation fuels, including electric vehicles, advanced clean biofuels, and public transit to reduce our dependence on vulnerable oil supplies. These investments would also reduce carbon pollution responsible for climate change.

Currently, there is no independent analysis that predicts that energy security and fuel prices would remain unchanged after the removal of the crude oil export ban. President Obama and Congress should not trade away our enhanced gasoline price stability and energy security. Instead, you should join together to defend the ban on crude oil exports.

End Notes

[1] *Energy Policy and Conservation Act*, Public Law 94-163, 94th Cong., 1st sess. (December 22, 1975), available at http://thomas.loc.gov/cgi-bin/bdquery/z?d094:SN00622:@@@L&summ 2=m&.

[2] Energy Information Administration, *AEO2014 Early Release Overview* (U.S. Department of Energy, 2014), Figure 12, available at http://www.eia.gov/forecasts/aeo/er/early_ production.cfm.

[3] Lawrence Kumins, "West Coast and Alaska Oil Exports" (Washington: Congressional Research Service, 2013) available at http://assets.opencrs.com/rpts/RS22142_20060525.pdf.

[4] Ibid.

[5] Bradley Olson and Dan Murtaugh, "Falling Gasoline Hurts Exxon Plea for U.S. Crude Exports," *Bloomberg Business Week,* January 28, 2014, available at http://www.

bloomberg.com/news/2014-01-28/falling-gasoline-hurts-exxon-plea-for-u-s-crude-exports-energy.html.

[6] Ibid.

[7] Energy Information Administration, "Light Louisiana Sweet (LLS) crude oil now sells at a historically large discount to Brent," This Week in Petroleum, December 11, 2013, available at http://www.eia.gov/oog/info/twip/twiparch/2013/131211/twipprint.html. .

[8] Energy Information Administration, "U.S. Imports by Country of Origin," available at http://www.eia.gov/dnav/pet/pet_move_impcus_a2_nus_ep00_im0_mbblpd_a.htm (last accessed January 2014).

[9] Energy Information Administration, *Short-Term Energy Outlook Supplement: EIA Estimates of Crude Oil and Liquid Fuels Supply Disruptions* (U.S. Department of Energy, 2013), available at http://www.eia.gov/forecasts/steo/special/pdf/2013_sp_05.pdf.

[10] Commission on Energy and Geopolitics, "Oil Security 2025: U.S. National Security Policy in an Era of Domestic Oil Abundance" (2014), available at http://secureenergy.org/sites/default/files/Oil_Security_2025_0.pdf.

[11] Daniel J. Weiss, "Big Oil's Lust for Tax Loopholes: Oil Prices and Profits Rise While Big Oil Defends Its Tax Loopholes," Center for American Progress, January 31, 2011, available at http://www.americanprogress.org/issues/green/news/2011/01/31/8951/big-oils-lust-for-tax-loopholes/.

[12] Energy Information Administration, "Exports," available at http://www.eia.gov/dnav/pet/pet_move_exp_dc_NUS-Z00_mbbl_m.htm (last accessed January 2014).

[13] Clare Foran, "AFL-CIO President Opposes Lifting Ban on Crude-Oil Exports," *National Journal,* January 14, 2014, available at http://www.nationaljournal.com/energy/afl-cio-president-opposes-lifting-ban-on-crude-oil- exports-20140114.

[14] Energy Information Administration, "Energy Consumption by Sector and Source, United States, Reference Case," available at http://www.eia.gov/oiaf/aeo/tablebrowser/#release=AEO2013&subject=2-AEO2013&table=2-AEO2013&region=1-0&cases=ref2013-d102312a (last accessed January 2014).

INDEX

#

21st century, 56

A

access, 14, 29, 32, 51, 57
Administrative Procedure Act, 34
agencies, 12, 35
air quality, 31
airline industry, 62
Alaska, 8, 10, 12, 66, 68
Alaskan North Slope, 10, 39
ANS, 39
arbitrage, 45, 49
armed conflict, 44
Asia, 33, 46, 49
assessment, 45
assets, 12, 20, 27, 68
atmospheric pressure, 5
authority, 9, 35, 42

B

ban, 45, 56, 59, 61, 62, 63, 65, 66, 68, 69
Barbados, 37
barriers, 27, 43, 44, 56
benefits, 24, 26, 30, 43, 44, 46, 47, 51, 59, 63, 65
Bureau of Labor Statistics, 60
businesses, 59
buyer, 48

C

carbon, 16, 31, 50, 68
carbon atoms, 16
carbon emissions, 50
Caribbean, 57
cartel, 28
catalyst, 42
certification, 12
challenges, 3, 4, 21, 22, 30, 36, 52
chemical, 6, 42, 58
chemical properties, 6
Chile, 29
China, 37, 39, 48
City, 55
classification, 6, 7
clean energy, 50
climate, 30, 31, 68
climate change, 30, 31, 68
coal, 28, 50, 56
Coast Guard, 42
commercial, 44
commodity, 58, 65
communication, 40
competition, 58
competitive advantage, 26

competitors, 45
complexity, 49
configuration, 8, 17, 19
conflict, 44, 51
Congress, vii, viii, 1, 2, 4, 11, 23, 27, 32, 33, 34, 35, 36, 40, 41, 42, 62, 65, 68
consensus, 56
conservation, 29
construction, 50
consumers, 24, 25, 28, 44, 45, 51, 57, 58, 59, 62
consumption, 8, 23, 27, 32
contamination, 31
Continental, v, ix, 55
contradiction, 16
controversial, 39
convergence, 25
cooperation, 50
correlations, 45
cost, 21, 22, 24, 25, 41, 45, 57, 63
Costa Rica, 37
Cuba, 59
current account, 48
current account deficit, 48
customers, 22, 47, 48

D

deficit, 48
Delta, v, ix, 61, 63
Delta Air Lines, v, ix, 61
Department of Commerce, 5
Department of Energy, 48, 68, 69
destiny, 59
diesel fuel, 3, 7, 8, 25, 51, 57, 68
diluent, 52
diplomacy, 41, 47
directives, 35, 50
displacement, 45, 47
disposable income, 58
distillation, 5, 17, 18, 46, 52
distortions, 44, 58
distribution, 21, 50, 58
domestic industry, 29
domestic markets, 46
drinking water, 31

E

economic considerations, viii, 2
economic development, 33
economic disadvantage, 48
economic growth, 44
economic power, 26
economic theory, 23
economics, 20, 22, 32, 33, 60
EIA, vii, viii, 1, 2, 3, 7, 14, 15, 17, 18, 19, 22, 24, 25, 28, 30, 36, 37, 38, 40, 41, 42, 51, 67, 69
embargo, vii, 1, 4, 39, 41, 56, 59, 62, 65
emergency, 9, 25, 27, 50
employment, 58
energy, viii, 3, 26, 27, 28, 29, 41, 43, 44, 45, 46, 47, 48, 49, 50, 53, 55, 56, 57, 58, 59, 61, 63, 65, 66, 68, 69
Energy Information Administration, vii, 1, 3, 5, 13, 14, 15, 16, 18, 19, 38, 39, 40, 41, 51, 64, 65, 66, 67, 68, 69
Energy Policy and Conservation Act, vii, 1, 4, 6, 9, 56, 65, 68
energy prices, 45
energy security, viii, 3, 41, 46, 59, 65, 68
energy supply, 44, 47
enforcement, 9
environment, viii, 3, 30, 33
environmental issues, 29, 30
EPCA, vii, 1, 4, 6, 8, 9, 10, 32, 34, 35, 42
equipment, viii, 2, 6, 19, 52, 58
EU, 29, 50
Europe, 24, 45, 46, 47, 49, 50, 57, 62, 63
European Union, 29
execution, 9
executive branch, 32, 34
executive order(s), 9, 12, 35, 39
exercise, 9
exhaustible natural resources, 29
export control, 35, 39
export restrictions, vii, viii, 1, 2, 3, 4, 5, 13, 14, 16, 17, 29, 30, 31, 32, 33, 35, 36, 39, 42, 56, 57, 58

exported oil, viii, 2, 23
exporter(s), 8, 12, 13, 25, 26, 27, 48, 50, 60
exports, vii, viii, ix, 1, 2, 3, 4, 5, 6, 8, 9, 10, 11, 12, 13, 14, 15, 16, 23, 24, 25, 26, 27, 29, 32, 33, 34, 35, 36, 39, 40, 41, 42, 43, 44, 45, 46, 47, 48, 49, 50, 52, 55, 56, 58, 59, 62, 65, 66, 68, 69
extraction, vii, 1, 3, 6, 30, 31, 32, 63

F

families, 68
fear, 50
federal law, 6, 56
federal regulations, 59
feedstock(s), 7, 8, 22, 38, 51, 52
financial, 45, 47, 48, 68
financial reports, 68
flour, 57
Ford, 7, 14, 15, 16, 18, 19, 22, 41
forecasting, 46
foreign investment, 44
foreign policy, 9, 43, 47, 49
formation, 15, 16, 62
free trade, 28, 29, 43, 45, 48, 50, 56
freedom, 53
fuel prices, 68

G

GATT, 28
GDP, 48, 58, 59
General Agreement on Tariffs and Trade, 28
geographic location, viii, 2, 13
geology, 31
global climate change, 50
global demand, 46, 57
global economy, 47, 50
global leaders, 59
global markets, 32, 62, 63
government revenues, 58
governments, 29, 58
GPS, 60
grades, 23, 57
gravity, 7, 16
greenhouse, 31
greenhouse gas(s), 31
gross domestic product, 48
groundwater, 31
growth, vii, viii, 2, 3, 13, 21, 41, 43, 46, 57, 59, 65
guessing, 49
guidance, 9
Gulf Coast, viii, 2, 6, 18, 21, 39, 51, 63
Gulf of Mexico, 36, 46

H

health, 48
heating oil, 8, 45, 62
heavy oil, 46
history, 22, 23, 39, 44, 47, 63
horizontal drilling, vii, 3, 55, 56, 57, 58
human, 29
human health, 29
hydraulic fracturing, vii, 3, 31
hydrocarbon(s), viii, 2, 5, 16, 17, 36, 38, 49, 51, 56

I

ideal, 50
IEA, 28
imports, vii, 2, 3, 19, 20, 26, 27, 33, 38, 41, 44, 46, 47, 48, 50, 56, 62, 63, 65, 67
income, 60
independence, 55, 57, 59, 63
India, 37, 57
industry(s), viii, 2, 6, 14, 15, 17, 24, 27, 31, 33, 36, 40, 44, 51, 56, 57, 58, 61, 62
inefficiency, 26
inflation, 44
infrastructure, 3, 13, 17, 21, 22, 24, 30, 59
INS, 40
institutions, 48
International Energy Agency, 42, 56, 60
international relations, 41
international trade, viii, 3, 23, 28, 29, 44

investment(s), viii, 2, 6, 13, 17, 19, 33, 43, 46, 50, 52, 59, 68
Iran, 27, 41, 47
issues, vii, viii, 2, 4, 23, 30, 31, 36, 69
Italy, 37

J

Japan, 28, 29, 46, 47, 49
job creation, 24
justification, 13

K

Korea, 49
Kuwait, 50

L

labor force, 58
labor force participation, 58
Latin America, 6, 18, 45
laws, 4, 6, 26, 39, 42, 56, 58
laws and regulations, 6, 26
lead, 31, 48, 50, 52
legislation, 4, 10, 32, 56
light, vii, viii, 2, 3, 5, 6, 8, 14, 16, 19, 20, 24, 30, 32, 36, 38, 41, 46, 50, 52, 57, 59
light crudes, viii, 2, 6
liquefied natural gas, 29, 47
liquid fuels, 66, 68
liquid phase, 5, 16
liquids, 3, 4, 27, 46, 51, 67
longevity, 33
Louisiana, 15, 38, 42, 69
lower prices, 22, 24, 25, 33, 58, 63
LTO, vii, viii, ix, 2, 3, 4, 6, 13, 14, 15, 16, 17, 19, 20, 21, 22, 23, 24, 30, 31, 33, 35, 36

M

magnitude, viii, 2, 14, 16, 23, 24, 26, 30
majority, 13, 16
Malaysia, 29
manufacturing, 50, 57, 58
market access, 21
market share, 28
marketability, viii, 2
marketing, 38
marketplace, 56
materials, 8
matter, 27, 48, 58, 67
media, 51
membership, 28
metaphor, 63
Mexico, 15, 27, 29, 37, 45, 46, 48
Middle East, 27, 47, 48, 50, 60
military, 27, 48, 61, 67
modifications, 22
multidimensional, 23
multiplier, 58

N

NAFTA, 45
national emergency, 9
national security, 9, 43, 49, 59
natural disaster(s), 67
natural gas, 3, 4, 6, 16, 17, 27, 28, 40, 42, 43, 44, 45, 46, 47, 48, 50, 51, 53, 56
negotiating, 29, 48
New England, 50
New Zealand, 29
Nigeria, 19, 20, 27
North America, 20, 30, 40, 41, 60, 63
North Korea, 59
nuclear program, 48

O

Obama, 38
OCS, 12
officials, 56
oil embargo, vii, 1, 4, 39, 41, 56, 59, 62, 65

oil production, vii, viii, 1, 2, 3, 6, 13, 14, 15, 18, 22, 24, 25, 26, 27, 28, 30, 32, 33, 41, 45, 52, 58, 59, 65
oil sands, 50
oil spill, 30
Oklahoma, 15, 21, 55
oligopoly, 62
open markets, 43
operations, 13, 35
opportunities, 4, 19
optimization, 19
Outer Continental Shelf (OCS), 11, 40, 42
Outer Continental Shelf Lands Act, 11, 42
ownership, 20

P

Pacific, 29, 46
Panama, 37
PCA, 4
permission, 15
Persian Gulf, 48
Peru, 29
petroleum, vii, 1, 3, 4, 5, 7, 9, 10, 11, 12, 19, 21, 23, 25, 26, 27, 28, 38, 39, 40, 41, 42, 43, 46, 49, 51, 57, 60, 66, 67, 68, 69
pipeline, viii, 2, 8, 9, 10, 12, 20, 21, 24, 30, 40, 48, 50
policy, vii, viii, 3, 4, 5, 14, 17, 30, 31, 32, 35, 36, 43, 44, 49, 51, 52, 62
policy makers, 30
policy options, viii, 3, 17, 32, 35
politics, 41
pollution, 68
power plants, 56
president, vii, 1, 4, 6, 8, 9, 10, 11, 33, 34, 35, 36, 38, 39, 42, 44, 47, 51, 59, 68, 69
President Clinton, 10
President Obama, 51, 68
price changes, 23, 45
price controls, vii, 1, 4, 44
price effect, viii, 2, 23, 24, 25
price stability, 65, 68
principles, 28
producers, viii, 2, 4, 6, 13, 21, 24, 25, 28, 30, 32, 33, 46, 47, 55, 56, 57, 58, 67
product market, 8
profit, 17, 45, 49, 68
profit margin, 17, 45
project, 20, 27, 40, 48
propane, 8, 51
protection, 50
public interest, 48

Q

quality characteristics, viii, 2, 39
quotas, 29

R

rash, 56
raw materials, 29
reality, 56
refinery configurations, viii, 2, 13, 19, 22, 30, 33, 45
Reform, 39
regulations, 6, 8, 9, 11, 12, 13, 34, 35, 39, 56, 58
regulatory framework, vii, 4, 9
relaxation, 13
renaissance, 55, 56, 57
requirements, viii, 2, 3, 10, 11, 12, 19, 21, 35, 47
reserves, 11, 28
resolution, 11
resources, 13, 27, 28, 30, 43, 44, 49, 50, 56
response, 4, 42, 50, 56
responsiveness, 45
restoration, 42
restrictions, vii, viii, 1, 2, 3, 4, 5, 9, 12, 13, 14, 16, 17, 29, 30, 31, 32, 33, 34, 35, 36, 39, 42, 44, 49, 52, 56, 57, 58, 59
retail, 45, 51
revenue, 59
rights, 8, 10
risks, 31, 43
routes, 61

rules, 26, 46
Russia, 47, 49, 53

S

Saddam Hussein, 50
safety, 30, 50
sanctions, 27, 48
Saudi Arabia, 20, 27, 33, 41, 57, 59
savings, 45
scarcity, 4, 56
scope, 19, 22, 31, 35, 40
security, 50, 59, 68
self-sufficiency, 67
seller(s), 6, 58
Senate, ix, 41, 42, 43, 55, 61, 65
short supply, 9, 12, 34
shortage, 44
Sierra Club, 42
signals, 49
Singapore, 29, 37
SNAP, 12, 40
South America, 57
South Korea, 37, 47, 48
spare capacity, 25, 26
specifications, 26
spending, 66
stability, 26
stakeholders, 13, 17, 36
state(s), 17, 28, 35, 42, 47, 59, 62
statutes, 8, 10, 12, 32, 42
statutory authority, 35
storage, 50
Strategic Petroleum Reserve, 8, 12, 28, 47
subsidy(s), 29
sulfur, viii, 2, 7, 52, 57, 59
supplier(s), 20, 24, 27, 28, 47, 49, 53
supply disruption, 28, 32, 45, 65, 67, 68

T

tar, 5, 57
target, 31, 32, 41
taxes, 29
technology(s), vii, 1, 3, 12, 15, 44, 55, 56, 63, 65
temperature, 16, 31, 51
territory, 29
testing, 8, 12
tight oil, vii, viii, 1, 2, 3, 5, 13, 14, 15, 18, 19, 51, 59
time periods, 45
total product, 25
trade, 23, 26, 28, 29, 43, 45, 46, 47, 48, 57, 68
trade agreement, 48
trade deficit, 48
trade policy, 28, 43
trading partners, 44, 47, 49, 57
transactions, 9
transport, 31, 32, 40, 52, 62
transportation, viii, 2, 3, 10, 14, 21, 22, 30, 31, 40, 45, 68
transportation infrastructure, 21, 40
treatment, 28

U

U.S. crude oil, vii, 2, 3, 4, 5, 16, 20, 21, 23, 24, 26, 28, 30, 31, 33, 39, 42, 45, 49, 57, 62
U.S. Department of Commerce, 39
U.S. economy, 48
U.S. policy, 32
UK, 45, 53
United, vii, viii, 1, 2, 3, 4, 6, 9, 10, 11, 12, 14, 15, 17, 21, 23, 24, 26, 27, 28, 29, 31, 32, 33, 35, 41, 43, 44, 45, 46, 47, 48, 49, 50, 52, 56, 62, 65, 68, 69
United Nations, 31, 48
United Nations Framework Convention on Climate Change, 31
United States, vii, viii, 1, 2, 3, 4, 6, 9, 10, 11, 12, 14, 15, 17, 21, 23, 24, 26, 27, 28, 29, 32, 33, 35, 41, 43, 44, 45, 46, 47, 48, 49, 50, 52, 56, 62, 65, 68, 69

V

vacuum, 7
variables, 17, 30, 44
vehicles, 65, 68
Venezuela, 20, 27, 59
vessels, viii, 2, 12, 31, 41
veto, 40
Vice President, v, ix, 61
Vietnam, 29
volatility, 25, 46, 49, 50, 62, 63, 67
vulnerability, 47, 65

W

war, 47
Washington, 47, 68
weather related events, 45
wells, 16, 31, 46, 56
West Africa, 51
wholesale, 51
Wisconsin, 40
workers, 63, 68
World Bank, 48
World Trade Organization (WTO), 4, 28, 29, 42
worldwide, 31
worry, 50

Y

yield, viii, 2, 7, 18, 22, 39, 52